AF334413

Nā Leo i ka Makani

Voices on the Wind

Members of a Hawaiian family stand in
front of their home. A throwing style fish net,
between two papaya trees, awaits use.
Circa 1890.
Photographer: Unknown.
Bishop Museum.

Nā Leo i ka Makani
Voices on the Wind

HISTORIC PHOTOGRAPHS OF HAWAIIANS OF YESTERYEAR

Text and Verse by Palani Vaughan

Art Direction by Bill Fong and Leo Gonzalez
Designed by Veronica Lam

MUTUAL PUBLISHING ✦ EDITIONS LIMITED

A hula dancer smiles proudly before the studio camera.
Honolulu, 1870.
Photographer: H.L. Chase.
Baker-Van Dyke Collection.

ISBN 0-935180-59-1

Voices on the Wind

Sons and daughters of these islands
Are you listening, to the voices of our *kūpuna*?
In the swirling winds high on ancient *pali*,
Hear them, feel their love.

Hear the voices on the wind above the ocean
Carried from the whispering surf of timeless seas.
Chanting *mele* sacred to our native *ʻāina*,
And to the pride our nation once did see.

Can you hear the voices of our proud *kūpuna*
In the midst of this world's toil and strife?
Hear them beckoning to us, sisters and brothers.
E hoʻoikaika ʻo mākou! E hoʻoala hou ai!

Listen! Listen!
Hoʻolohe e nā kupa o ka ʻāina.
Hear the voices beckon rise once more, Hawaiʻi.
Arise in strength and purity and love.

Listen! Listen!
To the voices of our *kūpuna.*
Let the rising winds touch you *e nā kupa,*
And be one with them throughout this land we love.

Composed by Palani Vaughan

nowledge of the Hawaiian culture, particularly considering that prior to the nineteenth century, oral accounts were relied upon to transmit information, would be extremely limited without the availablity of dictionaries translating the language of old Hawai'i into English. We are thus fortunate to have available through the arduous labors of their authors two works upon which to draw. ■ By comparing word meanings compiled at two different points in time and perhaps from different perspectives, we are able to comprehend more fully Hawaiian life during the nineteenth century and earlier. We are also through such a comparison able to appreciate even more, the importance of language, in preserving and transmitting culture. ■ *Nā Leo i ka Makani—Voices on the Wind* is thus dedicated to the memory, contribution and scholarship of Lorrin Andrews, the author of *A Dictionary of the Hawaiian Language,* and Mary Kāwena Pūku'i and Samuel H. Elbert, co-authors of *Hawaiian Dictionary: Hawaiian-English/English-Hawaiian.* ■ It is based on these works that we have presented our discussion of what we felt were some of the key aspects of Hawaiian life. . .*ali'i,* nobility; *kūlanakauhale,* village; *'ohana,* family; and *anaina,* gathering. ■ Lorrin Andrews' *A Dictionary of the Hawaiian Language,* first published in Honolulu in 1865, was the first major work of its type. It is the descendant of a smaller dictionary published by Andrews in 1838. The 1865 revision was expanded to about 15,000 Hawaiian-English entries and about 4,000 English-Hawaiian entries. ■ Lorrin Andrews (1795–1868) was among the earliest New England missionaries to reach Hawai'i. His Lahainaluna School on the Island of Maui nurtured such scholars as the now-famous David Malo. Andrews produced millions of pages of printed Hawaiian. When he learned that his sponsor, the Mission Board of Boston, was receiving contributions from American slave owners, he resigned in protest. At his death in Honolulu in 1868, he was deeply mourned by Hawaiians. ■ Since its publication in 1957, the *Hawaiian Dictionary* by Mary Kāwena Pūku'i and Samuel H. Elbert has been the definitive and authoritative work on the Hawaiian language. There have been four printings; the most recent, which occurred in 1986, saw 3,000 new entries added to the Hawaiian-English section bringing the total number of entries to almost 30,000. ■ Mary Kāwena Pūku'i, in the course of her long career on the staff of the Bernice P. Bishop Museum, translated many Hawaiian legends, chants and archival materials. A great deal of what we know today about the Hawaiian culture can be attributed to her efforts. ■ Samuel H. Elbert, professor emeritus of Pacific languages and linguistics, has been the resident authority of Polynesian languages at the University of Hawai'i for more the thirty-five years.

While the concept of a book may be the creation of only one or two persons, its completion requires contributions and assistance from many individuals and organizations. This is expecially the case for a book such as *Nā Leo i ka Makani—Voices on the Wind,* which covers broad sweeps of history and combines photographs with textual materials. ■ The first debt due is to the early photographers of Hawai'i whose devotion, dedication and labor produced the images that are a vital contribution to our knowledge of Hawaiian history. Carrying heavy equipment over long distances without the aid of modern day conveniences, these men and women produced a bountiful legacy. ■ Thanks must also be given to the private and public collectors and collections of historic photographs. Maintaining files of photographs that are accessible to researchers requires hours spent identifying, preserving, restoring, cataloguing and archiving. Wherever possible, we have indicated our sources. In particular, much *mahalo* should go to Betty Lou Kam, Clarice Maurico and Lynn Ann Davis of the Bishop Museum, Robert and Gladys Van Dyke, and Mary Jane Knight of the Hawaiian Mission Children's Society. ■ Several present-day photographers were gracious enough to supply images for the last section of the book dealing with current times. These include Douglas Peebles, whose photographs of the governor's inauguration were made available through the courtesy of Momi Cazimero, Boone Morrison, Francis Haar and staff photographers of the Honolulu *Star-Bulletin* and the Honolulu *Advertiser.* ■ Helping to finalize the text and captions required the editorial assistance of Dr. Glenn Grant. Our historical knowledge of the pictures was helped considerably by Robert Van Dyke; and Dr. A. Grove Day generously allowed us to reproduce almost in their entirety, segments from his *History Makers of Hawai'i: A Biographical Dictionary.* ■ Galyn Wong and Niki McDaniel provided proofing assistance at crucial times. ■ Gratitude must also be extended to the keepers of the knowledge of yesteryear, including composers, chanters, scholars, writers and historians. Throughout the years, they have preserved and enlightened our understanding of Hawaiian culture. ■ And to the Hawaiians of today who conceived *Ho'olako*—the Year of the Hawaiian—the event which inspired the creation of the book. ■ Finally, I wish to acknowledge my parents, Mr. Frank Palani Vaughan, Sr., and Mrs. Nohealeimamo Kalāluhi Vaughan, happily married for nearly fifty years, for their faithful loving-support and counsel. And my loving grandmothers, Mary Keli'iolono Worthington Vasconcelles and Rebecca Ka'aumoana Lum Lung Vaughan, for love, support and the knowledge of yesteryear that they shared with me. ■ And I dedicate this to my wife and especially to my children: *"Nā pua mae'ole o ku'u pu'uwai a me hekumu pau'ole o ke aloha a me ke ola no'u"*—"The never-fading flowers of my heart and a never-ending source of love and life for me." — PALANI VAUGHAN

To assist the reader in pronouncing Hawaiian words used in this book, some basic points to remember follow:

Vowels: Are pronounced:
A . . . . .ah, as in "bah"
E . . . . ay, as in "bay"
I . . . . ee, as in "bee"
O . . . . .oh, as in "no"
U. . . . . .oo, as in "do"

Consonants are: H, K, L, M, N, P, W. Words such as *ke* are pronounced "kaye," or *he*, pronounced "hey."

Occasionally, accent marks appear over or before certain vowels of written Hawaiian words. The accent marks are (¯), called macron or in Hawaiian, *makona,* and ('), called *'okina* or *'u'ina,* which is a glottal stop.

The macron (¯) appears over a vowel, as in the name of King Kalākaua, to indicate that particluar vowel requires emphasis in pronounciation. Therefore, it should be pronounced Ka-LĀ-kaua.

The glottal stop (') appears before certain vowels as in the name of King Kalākaua's wife, Queen Kapi'olani. The glottal stop indicates a break in the vocal sounding of the affected vowel. Therefore, the queen's name should be pronounced Ka-PI'O-lani.

Table of Contents

DEDICATION
6

PRONUNCIATION OF HAWAIIAN
8

ACKNOWLEDGEMENTS
7

FOREWORD
13

PREFACE
15

INTRODUCTION
16

AUTHOR'S NOTE
18

CHAPTER ONE

Ali'i/Nobility
20

CHAPTER TWO

'Ohana/Family
46

Mākua/Parents
60

Kūpuna/Elders
66

Keiki/Children
76

Kāne a'me Wahine/Men and Women
92

CHAPTER THREE

Kūlanakauhale/Village Life
118

CHAPTER FOUR

Hui/Gatherings
134

'Ahahui/Hawaiian Societies
142

Mele a'me Hula/Music and Dance
152

Ana 'Aina/Cultural Celebrations
164

INDEX OF FAMILY NAMES
175

SELECTED BIBLIOGRAPHY
176

A family grouped around an outrigger canoe.
Hōnaunau, Kona, circa ?
Photographer: Theodore Kelsey.
June Gutmanis Collection.

Preceding Page: In traditional Hawaiian
fashion, the generations work together with
the children cleaning the taro while the
seated adults pound the poi.
Hilo, 1890.
Photographer: E.N. Hitchcock.
Baker-Van Dyke Collection.

The fabric of Hawaiian culture is rich and strong. In the Year of the Hawaiian, we commemorate not only the arrival of Hawaiians to our islands but their remarkable contribution to the land that they made home. We acknowledge as well that this race, which was near extinction a century ago, has made such a remarkable recovery. ■ The legacy is an enduring one. In the photographs which follow are pictorialized the people who created this legacy. These were the Hawaiians of yesteryear—farmers, fishermen, villagers, family people, princes and princesses, musicians, dancers, people of the land and people of the sea. ■ The photographs were selected from the best public and private collections. Although they may depict a time which has been lost, they also communicate a spirit which lives on dynamically and vitally. In the spirit of *Ho'olako,* we are enriched by the remembrance. ■ This collection is for all people who open themselves to the love of others and to the land. As we appreciate this publication, let us dedicate ourselves to the perpetutation of the meaning of *Ho'olako,* to enrich the generations ahead in the pride of our culture.

GOVERNOR JOHN WAIHE'E
Executive Chambers,
Honolulu, 1987.

Amid a lush foliage setting, a group of
young men, and women, in perhaps their
Sunday after-church clothes, assemble for
a photograph.
Circa 1895
Photographer: Alonzo Gartley.
Bishop Museum.

A straw hat and warm smile adorn a beautiful
young Polynesian face.
Circa 1905.
Photographer: Unknown.
Bishop Museum.

isual documentation provides a vital source of information about Hawai'i and its people as they existed in the past. The quest for such documentation has grown as the community has become more aware of how rapidly Hawai'i is growing and changing. The path often leads to Bishop Museum's Visual Collection where the museum collections of art, photography and moving images offer a view of Hawaiian lifestyles and culture during the last two hundred years. Here, historians and scientists have utilized pictorial material to help develop new ideas or to support already established thought. Professional genealogists, as well as individuals seeking knowledge about their family histories, have rejoiced in finding a special photograph that helps solve a puzzle. And other individuals have enjoyed and appreciated visual materials for aesthetic reasons. ■ After westerners reached Hawai'i in the late eighteenth century, views of these islands were shared with the world through the publication of sketches made by ship artists. ■ The early photographers continued this tradition of faithfully creating and distributing images of the people of Hawai'i and the land on which they lived. The challenges that faced early photographers were many. But determination prevailed, and soon there were calls for the *pa'i ki'i* (photographer) to visit even the rural areas of the islands. ■ These early image makers include, among others, scientists like K.P. Emory and L.R. Sullivan; hobbyists like Alfred Mitchell and Hugo Stangenwald; and enterprising commercial photographers like Ray Jerome Baker and James J. Williams. Each used the camera as a tool to capture special scenes on film and paper. Each had a different approach and purpose, but the combined results of their work present a good view of a Hawai'i and a culture that otherwise might easly have been forgotten. ■ Searching through a collection of historical photographs provides insight into Hawaiian culture. Lifestyles and traditions that have long since vanished have a kind of immortality when held in the chemical layers of a photographic print. Today, these "old pictures" have become educational tools that stimulate interest in the Hawai'i of old, the Hawai'i of our parents and grandparents. ■ The preservation and dissemination of visual records depicting Hawai'i and the Pacific has been an important goal for Bishop Museum's Visual Collection. Bishop Museum encourages the community to visit the Visual Collection and explore the photograph, moving image and art collections. The wealth of this collection is also shared with the community through its use in educational programs, in exhibitions and in publications such as this one. And in this way, the story of Hawai'i and her people is told.

BETTY LOU KAM
Collection Manager of the Visual Collection,
Bishop Museum.

A peaceful aura settles over the country villages of Hawai'i nei. Nestled *mauka*, or toward the mountains, at the foot of a steep amphitheater valley in the midst of rich vegetation, the Hawaiian village is comprised of several wooden houses, a few shelters for the horses and other livestock and the tall white spire of a New England-style church. The days are languid and hot; the star-filled evenings are warm with the pungent odor of flowering plants. ■ The sounds of the village reverberate with a mixture of ease, excitement, joy and prayer. The *keiki's* laughter mingles with the knowing sighs of the *kūpuna* who have heard so many children rejoice in youth. The *kāne*, the men, are active with shouts of direction to those working in the *lo'i*, irrigated terraces for taro, or mounting their steeds for ranch work in the hills. The *wāhine*, the women, noisily care for the infants, join in the village work or exchange stories as they sew the distinctive quilts that will earn them a worldwide reputation. When the village *'ohana*, or family, gathers for feasts, music, dance, or prayer, their voices are raised in rollicking laughter, melodious song, "talk story" or solemn concern. The values they share, the work they cooperatively enjoy, the celebrations and mournings they observe, all weave the fabric of Hawaiian life in those *mauka* villages beyond the confusion, competition and drive of another world. ■ The Hawai'i of those ancient villages is slowly slipping from grasp. Only in the remote regions hidden from progress or in the vivid memories of the elders can the sights, sounds, smells and tastes of that former era be discovered. Photographs can, however, evoke sentiments that, like the old and modern, arouse a sense of nostalgia and loss. The spirit yearns to be able to walk into the daguerreotypes and tintypes of yesteryear—to meet the people who stare out across time—to converse on their lives and values, to share their lifestyles, concerns and peacefulness and to grow from the knowledge they possessed of the islands of which they were an extension. ■ *Nā Leo i ka Makani—Voices on the Wind* is an opportunity for the people of Hawai'i to touch this older world through the beauty and mystery of photographs. With the images of children, parents, chiefs, villages and elders, the haunting words of their imperishable language has also been lifted so that their thoughts, feelings and visions may be intelligible to a modern audience far removed from these earlier times. ■ Language is more than a means of communication—it is the bond of a common world view and a mirror of cherished values and beliefs. The "voices on the wind" that are heard with the images of old is the essence of the Hawaiian language, the important concepts, words and names that were the heritage of the people of yesteryear. The importance of speaking the right words, the precision of pronunciation and the care taken to say that which is true and defendable marked that beauty of the written and verbal Hawaiian language. In the texts of Lorrin Andrew's first dictionary of the Hawaiian language and Mary Pūku'i and Samuel Elbert's modern work are the keys to understanding the

Hawaiian mind and character. The roots of language contained in the definitions of words leads the modern reader into the natural world of ancient Hawai'i, cloaked in mythology, religion and practical knowledge. The genius of the Hawaiian language is in essence its simple relation of human beings to their natural environment. ■ *Nā Leo i ka Makani—Voices on the Wind* is presented, then, to *pūlama ho'oilina*...."cherish the heritage." Whether native Hawaiian or Hawaiian-at-heart, all of Hawai'i's people are *ka ho'oilina*, beneficiaries of the treasured legacy that has been inherited from *ka po'e kahiko*, the people of old. ■ The Hawaiian people have come in 1987 to an important watershed in their history. Hawai'i has elected its first popularly chosen native Hawaiian governor. Culture, music, art and language have gained more appreciation, interest and understanding. Through the efforts of "Tommy" Kaulukukui, renowned football hero and elected trustee of the Office of Hawaiian Affairs, with the support of other native Hawaiians, 1987 was proclaimed by former Governor George Ariyoshi as the Year of the Hawaiian. As President of *Ho'olako 1987*, Kaulukukui has helped that organization promote several meaningful activities intended to *ho'olako*, or "to enrich," the meaning of being Hawaiian. ■ The photographic images, poetic verses and Hawaiian language insights contained within *Nā Leo i ka Makani—Voices on the Wind* are offered in the Year of the Hawaiian as a legacy to present and future generations so that they will have an understanding of what has been lost and what must be preserved. In touching the proud heritage of Hawai'i's *kūpuna*, the words, sentiments and love of their world will perhaps once again be heard on the winds of time.

"Ua hala nā kūpuna, a he 'ike kōli'uli'u wale nō kō keia lā, i nā mea i ke au i hope lilo, iō kikilo."

"The ancestors have passed on; today's people see but dimly times long gone and far behind."

—From *Place Names of Hawai'i*
by M. Pūku'i, S. Elbert and E. Mo'okini.

The Year of the Hawaiian means different things to many people. But to this writer, Hawai'i's celebration of the Hawaiian, *Ho'olako,* affords a quality moment to enrich our lives. Through discovery and rediscovery of the rich cultural heritage left by our ancestors, emerges a better understanding and a greater appreciation of our roots. ■ The celebration is a time to "cherish the heritage," *pūlama ho'oilina.* Whether native or Hawaiian-at-heart, we are all beneficiaries, *ka ho'oilina,* of the treasured legacy inherited from our Hawaiian forefathers. ■ And what better way to reflect on that legacy than through old photographs (and some of more recent vintage) similar to those found in old family albums closeted away in storage and brought out of their obscurity into the light again. When in April of 1987 the publishers brought this collection of nostalgic images appearing in this volume for me to review, they requested that "the pictures seem to be asking that a story be told . . ." and would I attempt to tell it. I was immediately reminded of the period in my life when I conducted research in Hawai'iana. I was then despairing and sad in my awareness that many Hawaiians had little or no interest in understanding Hawaiian culture or history, something I attributed to the need to survive in Hawai'i's highly competitive socioeconomic environment. Later, it also occurred to me that the indifference may have been a consequence of not knowing or understanding the Hawaiian language. It became my belief that ignorance of the language was making native Hawaiians strangers to their heritage and, sadly, more significantly, strangers to their *kūpuna,* ancestors. ■ The rude awakening of my own shortcomings in Hawai'iana caused me to undertake in-depth study of the Hawaiian language and to launch into broadly based research of Hawaiian history, culture and my own family genealogy. Through fifteen-plus years of study, I was drawn closer to my *kūpuna* and to the ways and times of old Hawai'i. ■ I was also inspired to compose and record a song that I hoped would encourage Hawaiians to become more aware of their language, personal family histories, and their *kūpuna.* Entitled "Voices on the Wind," the lyrics appealed to Hawaiians to feel the presence of the *kūpuna,* to sense the history of their time and pride in their *ali'i,* to cherish their legacy of music, dance, legend and lore, and to value the way of life that should always be remembered. Appropriately, I have chosen the song's name as the title of this book. ■ My frustration of the early 1970s is not as intense today. Hawaiian cultural awareness had increased with the advent of the Hawaiian cultural renaissance of the late 1970s that saw the repopularization of Hawaiian music and hula. ■ I am elated that the Year of the Hawaiian is producing more serious students of the Hawaiian language, particularly among children and native Hawaiians. ■ In one area, though, there is room for much improvement: our visitor industry. Here, Hawaiian-language music and Hawaiian hula for years have suffered a decline in acceptance. This perplexes me for, as a performer, my

efforts over the years to promote awareness of Hawaiian-language music, Hawaiian history, the Hawaiian monarchy and the hula have been well received. ■ My Hawaiian monarchy music, hula shows and concerts have been performed in showrooms, on *lūʻau* grounds and in ballrooms of major hotels throughout the state, at the J.F. Kennedy Center for the Performing Arts in Washington, D.C., and even in Tokyo, Japan. ■ On all occasions, I was amazed at how appreciative audiences mainly comprised of visitors were. I hope the visitor industry will aspire to share more of the rich heritage of the people of the land, this *ʻāina* called Hawaiʻi, which draws to its shores and fascinates, millions each year. Perhaps in *Nā Leo i ka Makani—Voices on the Wind*, through verses and textual discourses on history, culture and language combined with historical photographs, the interest and awareness in the richness of the Hawaiian language, and other aspects of the culture will be rekindled. ■ Except where it was necessary to accommodate design and typography considerations, I have attempted to present the beauty of the Hawaiian language with the utmost accuracy, and by so doing, capture some of the beauty of the heritage. ■ *Hoʻolako* is a time to "cherish the heritage," *pūlama hoʻolina . . .*Whether native or Hawaiian-at-heart, we are all beneficiaries, *ka hoʻoilina,* of the treasured legacy we have inherited from our beloved Hawaiian ancestors.

A pāʻū rider on the jungle road to the volcano.
Hawaiʻi, 1890.
Photographer: E.N. Hitchcock.
Baker-Van Dyke Collection.

P. V.
Honolulu, 1987.

A L I ' I
Chiefly protector, noble aristocrat

P I ' O
Arching rainbow

L A N I
Reaching from heaven to earth
    Cherished in times of old

A L I ' I
Kind provider

M Ō ' Ī
Kingly ruler,
Benefactor of the people
    Cherished in times of old

A L I ' I
Dignified nobility
With chiefly hearts
And kind generosity
Remembered for their gifts
To Hawai'i's people
Enriching their lives
    In cherished times of old.

Composed by Palani Vaughan

CHAPTER ONE

Ali'i / Nobility

Monarchs of Hawai'i

KAMEHAMEHA I
1758?–1819

Liholiho
KAMEHAMEHA II
1796–1824

Kauikeaouli
KAMEHAMEHA III
1813–1854

Alexander Liholiho
KAMEHAMEHA IV
1834–1863

Lot Kapuaiwa
KAMEHAMEHA V
1830–1872

William Charles
LUNALILO
1833–1874

David
KALĀKAUA
1836–1891

Lydia Kamaka'eha Kaolomali'i
LILI'UOKALANI
1839–1917

T he chiefly class played an important role in the Hawaiian social system. The survival of the people of old depended in large measure upon the strength of the leadership which members of the *ali'i* class provided. ■ In the ancient times, the *ali'i*, chiefs, were said to be descended from the gods. The *maka'āinana*, commoners, revered these god-born leaders who guided their people with wisdom, strength and authority. So sacred were the *ali'i*, one could not step upon their shadows or gaze directly upon them without risking punishment. Adorned in their dramatic feather capes and helmets, often standing over six feet tall and weighing several hundred pounds, the *ali'i* possessed a nobility and pomp that was unsurpassed in the Pacific. ■ The word *ali'i* is defined by Pūku'i-Elbert as a "chief, chiefess, king, queen, noble; royal, kingly; to rule or act as a chief, govern, reign; to become a chief." The figurative interpretation is "kind." Sometimes *ali'i* was shortened to *li'i*. Thus, *ke ali'i* became *keli'i* in the singular form of chief and *nā ali'i* became *nāli'i* in the plural form. The *ke ali'i* or *keli'i* was the kingly or queenly ruler, the chiefly protector, the kindly provider. There was, in ancient days, ranking among *ali'i*—the lesser rank served under the primary chief with responsibilities which included governing and managing smaller land areas and the people on them within their sovereign domain. Not all sovereigns were the highest chiefs of the land. However, all *ali'i* were treated as exalted beings. In the symbolic poetry and chants of the people, Pūku'i-Elbert notes that the chief was signified by references to rain, mist, rainbow, hawk, cliff or great height. ■ The rainbow was perhaps the most dramatic symbol of the *ali'i* of highest rank. *Pi'o* is a word that implies the presence of a rainbow and also designates a particularly high rank in the *ali'i* hierarchy. *Pi'o*, according to Pūku'i-Elbert, means "to arch, of a rainbow." It appeared in the name of the wife and Queen of Kalākaua, Hawai'i's seventh king. Her name was Kapi'olani, which is translated by Pūku'i-Elbert to mean "the heavenly arch." ■ *Lani* was another term used frequently to describe the aristocrats of Hawaiian society. According to Pūku'i-Elbert, it means "very high chief, majesty, royal, exalted, high-born" and literally translates "from heaven to earth." Chiefs described in this way were much sought after by rulers to enhance their courts or, in the case of female chiefs, to bear their royal offspring. ■ One of the best known and most powerful *ali'i* in the days of old was Kamehameha the Great. An impressively large man, standing six feet, five inches tall, Kamehameha the Great was the warrior king from Kohala, Hawai'i, who through successive conquests unified the separate island kingdoms under his Hawaiian rule. He was an intelligent sovereign who ruled his united kingdom wisely, heeded sensible advice and used good judgment in adopting measures to preserve his absolute power throughout his lifetime rule. ■ In the establishment of his dynasty, Kamehameha the Great acquired several wives of high rank who bore him many children. One of the highest ranking of his wives was

Keōpūolani, who bore Kamehameha two sacred sons. Ka-lani-nui-kua-liho-liho-i-ke-kapu was the king's eldest son who later became Kamehameha II. Pūku'i-Elbert translates his name as "The Great Chief with the Burning Back— Taboo!" His chiefly rank was so sacred and elevated that if Liholiho had accidentally entered his father's *hale*, or thatched house, then ancient law would have required that the *hale* be destroyed by fire. ■ Another wife of Kamehameha was the powerful and influential Ka'ahumanu. Following the death of Kamehameha on May 18, 1819, Ka'ahumanu continued to wield power as *Kuhina Nui*, or Premier, a position which entitled her to share executive powers with the succeeding kings, Kamehameha II and Kamehameha III. It was a title position which had been created, it was said, by the old conqueror on his death bed. ■ Wearing the yellow-feathered cloak and feather-covered war helmet of the late king as emblems of her new office, Ka'ahumanu enjoyed her status as *Kuhina Nui* until her death thirteen years later on June 5, 1832. During those years, Ka'ahumanu was instrumental in influencing the young King Kamehameha II in leading the nation in the overthrow of the ancient gods and religious beliefs of old Hawai'i. The *Kuhina Nui* also helped Boston missionaries promote and establish Christianity in the Hawaiian kingdom. ■ The office of *Kuhina Nui,* a lifetime position, survived until 1864 when, during the reign of Kamehameha V, it was abolished. The *ali'i* who succeeded Ka'ahumanu as *Kuhina Nui* was High Chiefess Kīna'u (1832–1839), daughter of Kamehameha I by High Chiefess Kaheiheimālie and therefore half-sister to Kamehameha II and III. Kīna'u was also the mother of the future kings Kamehameha IV and V and of her eventual successor, the last *Kuhina Nui*, Victoria Kamamalu, who served from 1857 to 1864. ■ Other appointments to the *Kuhina Nui* post included Kīna'u's half-sister, Chiefess Kekāuluohi (1839–1845), the mother of future King Lunalilo. She was followed by Keoni Ana (1845–1857), son of John Young, one of Kamehameha the Great's British allies and a trusted counselor. ■ Other *ali'i* who assisted the sovereign in ruling the Kingdom were appointed governors to administer over each island. One such *ali'i*, Ka'ahumanu's brother, High Chief Kuakini, served as governor of the Island of Hawai'i and as acting governor of O'ahu. He was an imposing figure of a man, reportedly seven feet tall and weighing five hundred pounds. ■ The longest reigning *ali'i* of the Kamehameha line was the second son of Kamehameha, Kauikeaouli or Kamehameha III. At the time of Kamehameha III, the dramatic word *mō'ī* became frequently used to refer to the ruling sovereign. Pūku'i-Elbert translates *mō'ī* as "king, sovereign, ruler, queen." It is possible that this term was derived from two root words. The first of these is probably *mo*, short for *mo'o*, which according to Pūku'i-Elbert means "succession, series, especially of genealogical lines." Pūku'i-Elbert suggests that the second root word *'i* means "supreme, great." It was logical, then, that *mō'ī* should have been used to refer to the third absolute sovereign in the genealogical line of the Kamehamehas. ■ In response to the growing influence of western thinking in his kingdom, *Mōʻī* Kamehameha III, with admirable grace, yielded his power as absolute sovereign by changing his status to that of constitutional monarch when he gave Hawaiʻi its first written constitution on October 8, 1840. By that instrument, the King granted the common people new rights and a new voice in government through delegate representation in a legislative assembly comprised of commoners and high chiefs. Perhaps Kamehameha's greatest gift to the people was the Great Māhele of 1848, wherein the Kingdom's land was divided into two parts: the Crown Lands of Kamehameha III and the Government Lands which were given to the chiefs and to the people forever. ■ Hawaiʻi's constitutional monarchy continued through the reigns of Kings Kamehameha IV and V, Lunalilo and Kalākaua until its ill-fated fall in 1893 during the rule of King Kalākaua's sister and heir, Queen Liliʻuokalani. ■ The *aliʻi* of the nineteeth century had evolved into a new style of Hawaiian monarch. The feathered cloaks and helmets were exchanged for Victorian uniforms and medals. The grass-thatched *hale aliʻi* were eventually replaced with the elegant style of ʻIolani Palace. The feasts of old gave way to the state dinners on fine china dishes. The pomp and circumstance of the Hawaiian kings matched that of the royalty of England and France.■ Although the Hawaiian monarchy and Kingdom have passed from existence, it is fitting in the Year of the Hawaiian that the *aliʻi* and the legacies of *aliʻi* kindness left by the early Hawaiian rulers and by the *mōʻī* of the late Hawaiian Monarchy are recognized and not forgotten. ■ From Kamehameha the Great's "Law of the Splintered Paddle" to Kamehameha III's *Ua Mau Ke ʻEa O Ka ʻĀina I Ka ʻPono,* from Queen's Hospital established by Kamehameha IV to Lunalilo Home for elderly Hawaiians lovingly created by King Lunalilo, from Kapiʻolani Maternity Hospital founded by Queen Kapiʻolani to King Kalākaua's ʻIolani Palace and to *Aloha ʻOe* composed by Queen Liliʻuokalani, the royalty contributed immeasurably to the the enrichment of the lives of their subjects. Their gifts to their people will long be cherished.

Kamehameha I wearing the famed "red vest."
Drawn from life by Choris, 1816.
Baker-Van Dyke Collection.

(1758?–1819) "The Lonely One," the chief who first united all the main islands under one rule, was born in North Kohala. It is certain that his mother was Keku'i'apoiwa, though historians debate whether his father was King Kahekili or High Chief Keōua ■ By the time Kamehameha's uncle, Kalaniopu'u, became ruler of Kohala, the young man was a celebrated warrior. Through military victories beginning on the Big Island in 1782 and ending on O'ahu in 1795, he established his rule over all the islands which he united. (Kaua'i was obtained by agreement.) ■ Kamehameha I, founder of the dynasty that was to last until 1872, died on May 8, 1819, at Kailua, Hawai'i, where he had set up his court in 1811. All his life he had been loyal to the religion of his ancestors. However, when the priests told him that a human sacrifice was demanded at his death, he refused, saying: "The men are kapu for the king"—meaning that his followers should live to serve his son Liholiho, who would succeed him on the throne as Kamehameha II. The bones of the father, as was customary, were taken and concealed in a secret cave. "Only the stars of the heavens know the resting place of Kamehameha." ■ (from A. Grove Day, "History Makers of Hawaii")

Ka'ahumanu, a wife of Kamehameha I, as Premier or *Kuhina Nui*.
Sketched from life by Choris, 1816.
Baker-Van Dyke Collection.

Kamāmalu (1802–1824) was a daughter of Hoapili and Kalakua and a sister of Kekāulohi and Kīna'u. The favorite wife of Kamehameha II, she accompanied him to London and died there a few days before his own death.
Portrait drawn from life by John Hayter.
London, 1824.
Baker-Van Dyke Collection.

Kamehameha II.
Drawn from life by John Hayter.
London, 1824.
Baker-Van Dyke Collection.

KAMEHAMEHA II

Son of Kamehameha I by Keōpūolani, Liholiho (1796–1824) was somewhat spoiled at the court. When his father died in the critical year 1819, Liholiho was told by the favorite queen, Ka'ahumanu, that by the will of Kamehameha I she was to jointly rule the kingdom as Kuhina Nui or Premier. Liholiho and his advisers soon overthrew the ancient kapu system by having men and women of the court eat at the same table. At the end of this ceremony, he announced that the heiau temples should be destroyed and all the old idols overthrown. ■ *Liholiho believed, like his father, that his kingdom was under the protection of Great Britain, and decided to visit London with his favorite wife Kamāmalu, Governor Boki of O'ahu and his wife Liliha, Kekūanaō'a, several other chiefs, and his secretary, a Frenchman named John Rives. Sadly, while abroad, his party was attacked by a disease unknown to them—measles. Kamāmalu died on July 8. Liholiho, stricken with grief as well as the disease, died on July 14.* ■ *(from A. Grove Day, "History Makers of Hawaii")*

KA'AHUMANU

(1768?–1832) This powerful chiefess was born at Hana, Maui, daughter of the elder Ke'eaumoku and Nāmāhana. Her brothers were Ke'eaumoku II and Kuakini (Cox). She became one of the wives of Kamehameha I when he was the ruling chief of the Island of Hawai'i. A breach between the pair was healed by Captain George Vancouver in 1793. ■ *As foster mother of Kamehameha II she was named co-ruler with him and became the first Kuhina Nui, or Regent. She led him in the celebrated breaking of the ancient religious tabu. In 1821, when King Kaumualii of Kaua'i was brought to Honolulu as a virtual hostage, he was married to Ka'ahumanu, who also married the king's heir, Keali'iahonui. She was left in charge of the kingdom when the royal party left for London in 1823. Six months after Kamehameha II departed for England, Ka'ahumanu proclaimed a code of civil laws, clearly based on missionary teaching. It is said that she ruled her people with "a rod of iron."* ■ *(from A. Grove Day, "History Makers of Hawaii")*

Nāhiʻenaʻena (Harriet Keōpūolani) (1815–
1836) was the daughter of Kamehameha I
and his kapu wife Keōpūolani, and sister
of Kamehameha II and Kamehameha III.
Princess Nāhiʻenaʻena was the darling of the
court and was educated by the American
missionaries. In 1824, the year following the
departure of her brother Kamehameha II for
England, she reverted to the belief in the
ancient deities, and the conflict between two
clashing doctrines disturbed her throughout
her short life. She was excommunicated by
the Protestants in May, 1835. Many of the
chiefs felt that she should marry her brother,
Kamehameha III, to concentrate the royal
blood, but this Hawaiian custom was op-
posed by the Christians. In November, 1835,
she married the high chief LeleiōHoku and
in September of the following year gave birth
to a stillborn son. Nāhiʻenaʻena died a few
months later at the age of twenty-one. (from
A. Grove Day, *History Makers of Hawaii*)
Drawn from life by Dampier, 1825.
Baker-Van Dyke Collection.

Miriam ʻAuhea Kekāuluohi (1794?–1845)
was a daughter of Hoapili and Kalakua and
a sister of Queen Kamāmalu and Kīnaʻu.
Brought up at Kahuluʻu, Oʻahu, by her grandparents, Keʻeaumoku and Nāmāhana, in
1809 she became one of the five wives of
Kamehameha I and at his death became a
wife of his son, Kamehameha II. She married
Kanaʻina in 1834 and bore a male child, the
future King Lunalilo.

Miriam was a stern chiefess but an over-
indulgent mother. She loyally supported the
Royal School of the Protestant missionaries
but was equally tolerant of other faiths.
She succeeded Kīnaʻu as *Kuhina Nui* from
1839 to 1845. (from A. Grove Day, *History
makers of Hawaii*)
Engraving by Agate of the United States
Exploring Expedition, 1840.
Baker-Van Dyke Collection.

Kuakini (John Adams) (1791–1844),
youngest son of Keʻeaumoku and Namahana
and brother of Kaʻahumanu, was also known
as Kuakiniokalani or Kuakinikona-hale. He
was a high chief and governor of the Island of
Hawaiʻi from 1820 until his death. He was
one of the first chiefs to read and write
English and Hawaiian. He became acting
governor of Oʻahu in 1831 and was a diligent
supporter of missionary ideals. Kuakini built
a fort at a site near the offical temple of
Kamehameha I and armed it with cannon.
He also built many schools and a large
meeting house near the mission at Waimea,
Hawaiʻi. (From A. Grove Day, *History Makers
of Hawaii*)
Sketch by William Ellis, 1822.
Baker-Van Dyke Collection.

Boki (?–1830?) was the son of Kuamanohā, a chief of Maui, and was a younger brother of Kalanimoku. His original name was Kamāʻuleʻule; his nickname came from a variation on Boss, the name of the favorite dog of Kamehameha I. ■ Boki was appointed governor of Oʻahu and confirmed in his post by Kamehameha II. He agreed to the breaking of the tabus in 1819 and accepted the Protestant missionaries arriving in 1820, although he had been baptized as a Catholic. ■ Boki became resentful of the power of Kaʻahumanu and her missionary advisers, and not surprising, allied himself with foreigners. ■ (from A. Grove Day, "History Makers of Hawaii")

LILIHA

Liliha (?–1842) was the daughter of Hoapilikāne and a granddaughter of Kalola. She was the wife of Boki and accompanied him to England in 1823. After his departure on a voyage to the South Pacific, she succeeded him as governor of Oʻahu. Later, however, the chiefs decided to put Oʻahu under Kaʻahumanu. Liliha then retired to Lāhainā, Maui, but remained the center of the anti-missionary faction. In 1839, during the "Great Revival," Liliha was converted to the Protestant faith, along with many other chiefs. ■ (from A. Grove Day, "History Makers of Hawaii")

Boki and Liliha. This is the original sketch as presented to Queen Emma in London in 1865, by the artist.
Drawn from life by John Hayter.
London, 1824.
Van Dyke Collection.

Kauikeaouli (1813–1854), the ruler who held the throne of the islands for the longest reign in history, was a son of Kamehameha I and Keōpūolani and a younger brother of Kamehameha II. He was nine years old when his brother left for England, naming him heir to the monarchy, and was proclaimed king in 1825 under a regency with Ka'ahumanu as Kuhina Nui, who was later succeeded by his half-sister Kīna'u. ■ *During his reign, the Hawai'i Kingdom began to come to grips with the problems caused by the increasing settlement of foreigners. The tax system was reformed and there occurred the first legal basis for land ownership.* ■ *Kamehameha III married Kalama on February 14, 1837, but they were childless, and at his death, the throne was occupied by his named successor, his younger nephew Alexander Liholiho, who became Kame-hameha IV.* ■ *(from A. Grove Day, "History Makers of Hawaii")*

Kauikeouli, King Kamehameha III and his consort Queen Kālama.
Depicted by A. Plum, artist of the *Voyage of the Galathea*, 1845, 1856, 1847, on behalf of the Danish Government.
Van Dyke Collection.

Hakaleleponi Kapakuhaili Kālama (1817–1870) was born near Kailua, Kona. The daughter of Naihekukui, she began the longest reign of a Hawaiian queen on February 14, 1837, when the Reverend Hiram Bingham married her to Kamehameha III. She took part in the many events of his reign.

Son of Mataio Kekūanaōʻa and Kīnaʻu, grandson of Kamehameha I, Alexander Liholiho (1834–1863) was the younger brother of Lot Kamehameha (Kamehameha V) and elder brother of Victoria Kamāmalu. ■ *He was proclaimed king at the death of his uncle, Kamehameha III, in December, 1854.* ■ *He was concerned about the decimation of his subjects by disease, and on April 20, 1859, signed a law setting up a hospital in Honolulu for sick and destitute Hawaiians. Along with Emma, he personally solicited funds to erect Queen's Hospital.* ■ *The king was an intelligent and articulate gentleman, fluent in both English and Hawaiian, and translated into the latter language the English Book of Common Prayer. British influence in the kingdom revived under his reign.* ■ *Weakened by asthma and sorrow over the death of his son a year before, Alexander Liholiho died on November 30, 1863, at the age of twenty-nine, and was succeeded by his elder brother.* ■ *(from A. Grove Day, "History Makers of Hawaii")*

Alexander Liholiho, Kamehameha IV. 1862. Younger brother of Lot, he was adopted by Kamehameha III and thus became heir to the throne.
Artist: Unknown.
Van Dyke Collection.

At birth, the future Queen Emma (1836–1885) was given the name of Kalanikaumakeamano; after the death of her husband and son she took the name of Kaleleonālani. Emma was the great-grand-daughter of Keliʻimaikaʻi, full brother of Kamehameha I. Her parents were George Naeʻa and Fanny Kakelaokalani Young. As a child, Emma was adopted by her maternal aunt, Grace Kamaʻikui Young Rooke.

Emma was married on June 19, 1856, to Kamehameha IV and shared the experiences of his reign. She took outstanding roles in the founding of the Queen's Hospital, named for her. The couple shared the introduction of the Episcopal Church in Hawaiʻi. Emma also sponsored the founding of St. Andrew's Priory, a school for girls.

When King Lunalilo died in 1874 without naming a successor, she unsuccessfully sought election as monarch. (from A. Grove Day, *History Makers of Hawaii*)
Lithograph by Adolph Ekelöf, in 1872
Van Dyke Collection.

Son of Mataio Kekūanaōʻa and Kīnaʻu, Lot Kapuaiwa Kamehameha (1830–1872) was four years older than his brother Kamehameha IV, and like him, was to reign for nine years. ■ *When Kamehameha IV died on November 30, 1863, Lot was immediately proclaimed his successor. Kamehameha V has been called "the last great chief of the olden type." He believed that the example of his grandfather, Kamehameha I, gave him the right to lead the Hawaiian people personally, and favored a stronger monarchy that verged on despotism. He was, however, a kindly despot, and wanted to protect his subjects from waste and idleness.* ■ *Kamehameha V was known as "the bachelor king." His sister, Victoria Kamāmalu, was named as his successor, but she died in 1866. An hour before his death on December 11, 1872, Lot called Bernice Pauahi Bishop to his bedside and asked that she become his successor, but she modestly declined this offer.* ■ *The decision of Kamehameha V not to name a successor to the throne resulted in invoking the constitutional provision for electing kings of Hawaiʻi.* ■ *(from A. Grove Day, "History Makers of Hawaii")*

Lot Kamehameha, King Kamehameha V.
Honolulu, 1867.
Photographer: Henry L. Chase.
Baker-Van Dyke Collection.

William Charles Lunalilo (1833–1874) was a chief of high ancestry. He was a grandson of a half-brother of Kamehameha I. His parents were Charles Kanaʻina and Kekāuluohi, a sister of Kīnaʻu. ■ *When Kamehameha V died without naming a successor, the Constitution provided that the throne should be filled by a vote of legislators. Lunalilo, the outstanding survivor of the royal line, offered himself as a candidate. The voters on January 1, 1873, were almost unanimous in favor of "Prince Bill," and he took the throne on January 8.* ■ *After a serious case of tuberculosis, he died in Honolulu on February 3, 1874, a little more than a year after his election. Lunalilo is best remembered as the first Hawaiian to leave his property to a work of charity. His will created Lunalilo Home, "for the use and accommodation of poor, destitute, and infirm people of Hawaiian blood or extraction, giving preference to old people."* ■ *(from A. Grove Day, "History Makers of Hawaii")*

Prince William Charles Lunalilo, just before becoming king.
Honolulu, 1869.
Photographer: Henry L. Chase.
Baker-Van Dyke Collection.

Left: Young Prince William Charles Lunalilo.
Honolulu, circa 1850.
Photographer: Probably Stangenwald.
Baker-Van Dyke Collection.

Konia (1807–1857), a granddaughter of
Kamehameha I, was the wife of Pākī and the
mother of Bernice Pauahi Bishop. She was a
member of the legislature from 1840 to 1847.

Abner Kaʻehu Pākī (1808–1855) was born
on Molokaʻi, a descendant of the Kameha-
mehanui and Kiwalaʻō families of Maui and
Hawaiʻi. He was the great-grandson of
Kekaulike. His father was Kalanihelemaiiluna
and his mother was Kuhoʻoheiheipahu. He
was captain of the fort at Honolulu in 1840
and a member of the national council. He was
at various time a Supreme Court judge,
member of the House of Nobles, acting
governor of Oahu, privy councillor, and
chamberlain to Kamehameha III. He was the
father of Bernice Pauahi Bishop, for whom in
1847 he built a large house in the center of
Honolulu. (from A. Grove Day, *History Makers
of Hawaii*)

Left: Princess Ruth Keʻelikōlani (Luka)
(1826–1883) was the daughter of Mataio
Kekūanaōʻa and Pauahi, a half-sister of
Kamehameha IV, Kamehameha V, and
Victoria Kamāmalu. Her first husband was
LeleiōHoku, son of Kalanimoku; one child
died in infancy and the other, William Pitt
Kīnaʻu (1842–1859), at the age of seventeen.
Ruth's second husband was Isaac Young
Davis, a grandson of Isaac Davis the British
sailor. A child of this couple died in infancy,
but Ruth adopted a young brother of David
Kalākaua and named him William Pitt
LeleiōHoku. When this heir died in 1877,
Ruth, who owned large estates and houses,
left most of her great wealth to Bernice
Pauahi. (from A. Grove Day, *History Makers
of Hawaii*)
  Princess Ruth Keʻelikōlani with Sam Parker
to left and John A. Cummins to the right.

Princess Pauahi (1831–1884) was born in Honolulu, a great-granddaughter of Kamehameha I. She was named Pauahi after an aunt whose daughter was Princess Ruth. At the age of eight, Bernice began attending Royal School along with other young people of the ruling group. She was married at the school in 1850 to Charles Reed Bishop. ■ *On the death-bed of Kamehameha V in 1872, he offered to name Bernice as his successor to the throne, but she declined.* ■ *At the death of Ruth in 1883, Bernice in-herited the bulk of her estate and thus became heiress to most of the Kameha-meha lands, totalling close to nine per cent of the area of the Hawaiian Islands. Her will established the endowed Kame-hameha Schools, to educate young people of Hawaiian blood, which opened the boys' division in 1887 and the girls' division in 1894.* ■ *(from A. Grove Day, "History Makers of Hawaii")*

Princess Bernice Pauahi Bishop.
Honolulu, circa 1870.
Photographer: Henry L. Chase.
Baker-Van Dyke Collection.

Kapiʻolani (1834–1899), a niece and namesake of the chiefess who defied Pele, was granddaughter of King Kaumualiʻi of Kauaʻi. Two of her sisters were Virginia Kapoʻoloku Poʻomaikelani and Esther Kinoiki Kekaulike (who married David Piʻikoi).

During her first marriage—to a chief named Bennett (Benet) Namākēhā—she acted as governess of the little Prince Albert. She married David Kalākaua in 1863 and was crowned with him in 1883 on the ninth anniversary of his accession to the throne.

Kalākaua and Kapiʻolani had no children. After his death, the queen dowager concerned herself with the welfare of Hawaiian women. She established and helped to support the Kapiʻolani Maternity Home and the Kapiʻolani Home for Leper Girls. (from A. Grove Day, *History Makers of Hawaii*)
Honolulu, 1883.
Photographer: J.J. Williams.
Baker-Van Dyke Collection.

Left: King David Kalākaua.
San Francisco, 1881.
Photographer: Taber.
Baker-Van Dyke Collection.

The future elected king was born in Honolulu at the foot of Punchbowl Crater. David Kalākaua (1836–1891) was not a member of the Kamehameha dynasty. His ancestors had been prominent chiefs on the Island of Hawaiʻi. His great-grandfather was Keaweaheulu, and he was one of the seven children of Kapaʻakea and his wife Keohokalole; two younger sisters were Liliʻuokalani and Likelike. ■ Defeated in 1872 during the election for the throne, he became monarch in the 1874 election to begin a reign that earned him the title of "The Merrie Monarch." ■ Kalākaua was the first king in history to visit the United States and was royally received. In 1881, he set out on a triumphant tour of the world to visit fellow heads of state. He conceived the idea of being publicly crowned, although no previous Hawaiian ruler had received such a ceremony. On February 12, 1883, the ninth anniversary of his election, in front of the fine new ʻIolani Palace whose cornerstone had been laid in 1879, Kalākaua, the elected king, placed a jeweled crown on his head and another on that of his queen. Two days later, the celebrated statue of Kamehameha I that still stands in front of Aliʻiolani Hale in downtown Honolulu was unveiled by the King. ■ In November 1890, Kalākaua, in poor health but seeking to achieve masonic shriner status, left for San Francisco, where he died on January 20, 1891. His body was brought to Honolulu by an American warship, and after a ceremonious lying-in-state, was buried in the Royal Mausoleum, leaving his younger sister Liliʻuokalani to ascend the throne. ■ (from A. Grove Day, "History Makers of Hawaii")

Above: King Kalākaua's departure on the *U.S.S. Benicia* to Washington, D.C., November 17, 1874, for reciprocity treaty negotiations with the United States Congress.
Honolulu, 1874.
Photographer: Unknown.
Bishop Museum.

King Kalākaua and his party at Kawaihae. The king is in the hammock. Maria Mālie Merseberg Kahaʻi is behind the coconut tree. John Cummins, dressed in white, is seated at right. James Boyd, with hat, is next to the coconut tree.
Kawaihae, Hawaiʻi, 1888.
Photographer: J.A. Gonsalves.
Bishop Museum.

Right: King Kalākaua and friends at a home on the South Kona coast.
Circa 1889.
Photographer: Unknown.
Bishop Museum.

William Pitt Kalahoʻolewa LeleiōHoku (1835–1877). Brother of two future rulers of the kingdom, LeleiōHoku was the youngest son of Kapaʻakea and his wife Keohokalole and brother of David Kalākaua and Lydia Liliuʻokalani. He was adopted at birth by Princess Ruth, who named him LeleiōHoku in memory of her first husband and made him heir to her large estate. He grew up to be a gifted poet and musician. Some of his compositions are still sung in the islands.

Soon after Kalākaua became king, he named LeleiōHoku as his successor. Sadly, he died of pneumonia on April 9, 1877, leaving Liliʻuokalani as the heir of her brother. (from A. Grove Day, *History Makers of Hawaii*)
Honolulu, 1876.
Photographer: H.L. Chase.
Baker-Van Dyke Collection.

LILI'UOKALANI

Last of the rulers of the Kingdom of Hawai'i, Lydia Kamaka'eha Kaolamali'i Lili'uokalani (1839–1917) was born in Honolulu, one of seven children of Kapa-'akea and his wife Keohokalole. Her great-grandfather was Keaweaheulu, who, she claimed, was first cousin to the father of Kamehameha I. The child was adopted by Paki and Konia and reared as foster sister to Bernice Pauahi. Lydia was two years younger than her brother Kalākaua, and she was also a sister Miriam Likelike, who was much of younger. Lydia attended the Royal School and had a good education. ■ *On September 16, 1862, Lili'uokalani married John Owen Dominis, who was made governor of the Island of O'ahu. The couple lived at his mother's home, Washington Place. She acted as regent of the Kingdom during the world tour of Kalākaua, and the childless king made his sister the heiress apparent on April 10, 1877, after the death of William Pitt LeleiōHoku. Lili'uokalani*

attended the jubilee of Queen Victoria of England with her sister-in-law Queen Kapi'olani in 1887. After the death of Kalākaua, Lili'uokalani was proclaimed Queen on January 29, 1891. Her desire to restore the old authority of the crown led to the downfall of that crown. Revolution was in the air, and her efforts to overthrow the Constitution of 1887 which she had taken an oath to maintain was only one of the complicated causes of the bloodless overthrow of the monarchy. Deposed on January 17, 1893, she continued to obtain support. When, during the counter-revolution of 1895, a small arsenal of arms and dynamite bombs was uncovered, she was confined in an upper room of her former palace. "Mrs. Dominis" under duress signed a formal abdication and pledged allegiance to the Republic of Hawai'i. Her efforts to be reseated on the throne were unsuccessful. ■ *(from A. Grove Day, "History Makers of Hawaii")*

Princess Lydia Kamaka'eha (Mrs. John Owen Dominis) at the time she officially becomes Princess Lili'uokalani, Regent, during the period when her brother King Kalākaua toured the world.
Honolulu, 1881.
Photographer: J.J. Williams.
Baker-Van Dyke Collection.

Right: A grand picture of Queen Lili'uokalani, deposed, taken just before her departure for Washington, D.C., to fight for her cause of the return of Hawai'i and its lands.
Honolulu, 1897.
Photographer: Davey.
Baker-Van Dyke Collection.

Princess Kaʻiulani with friends at her
ʻĀinahau Estate in Waikīkī.
Waikīkī, Honolulu, circa 1895.
Photographer: J.J. Williams.
June Gutmanis Collection.

KAʻIULANI

*Victoria Kawēkiu Kaʻiulani Lunalilo
Kalaninuiahilapalapa (1875–1899) was
born in Honolulu, daughter of Governor
Archibald Scott Cleghorn and Princess
Miriam Likelike and niece of King Kalākaua and Queen Liliʻuokalani. When
Kalākaua was in Japan on his world
tour in 1881, he proposed that Kaʻiulani,
then five years old, might in the future
marry a Japanese prince, to make a
royal alliance.* ■ *The princess was
widely loved as a linguist, musician,
artist, horsewoman and swimmer, and
was active in many charities. At the
accession of Liliʻuokalani, she was
proclaimed heiress apparent of the
Kingdom. After the overthrow of the
monarchy in 1893, Kaʻiulani went
to Washington, D.C., with Davies to
argue for the restoration of the throne.
She died on March 6, 1899.* ■ *(from A.
Grove Day, "History Makers of
Hawaii")*

Lili'uokalani is remembered as the author of
a number of songs. Pictured here is sheet
music to "Lili'uokalani's Prayer," composed
during her imprisonment by the Republic of
Hawai'i in 1895.
Baker-Van Dyke Collection.

Left: Princess Victoria Ka'iulani.
Honolulu, 1897.
Photographer: J.J. Williams.
Baker-Van Dyke Collection.

Queen Lili'uokalani, just after the overthrow
of the monarchy, in her garden at Washington
Place. To the rear, Colonel Sam Nowlein.
Honolulu, 1893.
Photographer: Severin.
Baker-Van Dyke Collection.

Queen Lili'uokalani has a relaxed moment
at the famed Cummins Ranch at Waimānalo,
O'ahu. To her rear: Prince David
Kawānanakoa and Prince Jonah Kūhiō
Kalaniana'ole. In front: Sam Parker and John
Cummins.
Waimānalo, 1892.
Photographer: J.A. Gonsalves.
Baker-Van Dyke Collection.

Right: Mrs. Hiram Kahanawai, sister of the
future Queen Kapi'olani. She then became
Princess Po'omaikelani. She was called
Mistress of the Royal Robes. Later, she was
governor of the Island of Hawai'i. When her
sister Kekaulike died, she brought up the
royal princes Kūhiō and Kawānanakoa.
Honolulu, 1868.
Photographer: Henry L. Chase.
Baker-Van Dyke Collection.

The magnificent Princess Elizabeth Kahanu Kalaniana'ole, wife of Prince Jonah Kūhiō Kalaniana'ole.
Circa 1913.
Photographer: Unknown.
Baker-Van Dyke Collection.

Prince Jonah Kūhiō Kalaniana'ole.
Honolulu, 1915.
Photographer: Bonine.
Hawai'i State Archives.

Prince Jonah Kūhiō Kalaniana'ole (1871–1922) was descended from the kings of Kaua'i; Kaumualii was his grandfather. Jonah was born at Kōloa, Kaua'i, on March 26, 1871. His parents were the high chief David Kahalepouli Pi'ikoi and Princess Kinoiki Kekaulike. He was a cousin of King Kalākaua and Queen Lili'uokalani and a nephew of Queen Kapi'olani, consort of Kalākaua. His elder brothers were Prince Edward Keli'iahonui (1869–1887) and Prince David Kawānanakoa. He and his brothers were made princes by royal decree when he was thirteen. ■ He was trained as a successor to the royal throne. But when he was twenty-one the monarchy was overthrown. He was arrested and charged with treason for his part in the counter-revolution of 1895 and served, not unhappily, as a political prisoner for about a year. He married Elizabeth Kahanu Ka'auwai, daughter of a chief of Kaua'i, in 1896. She was considered one of the must beautiful woman of her time. ■ As an elected Congressional delegate, he attained a number of political gains for Hawai'i during his long term, and is remembered best as the father of the present Hawaiian Homes Commission. ■ Kūhiō in 1903 organized the Order of Kamehameha and officiated at the first observance of Kamehameha Day in 1904. He also organized the Chiefs of Hawai'i and the Hawaiian Civic Club. He died on January 7, 1922, at the age of fifty, and was given the last state funeral held in Hawai'i for an ali'i. He was buried in the Royal Mausoleum. ■ (from A. Grove Day, "History Makers of Hawaii")

'OHANA

The family

KŪPA'A

Standing firm
Steadfastly loyal
One to the other,
Bonded by love and trust,
Each for the other

KŪPUNA

The respected elder grandparents

MĀKUA

The honored parents

KAMA, NA KEIKI

The children

MO'OPUNA

Seeds for the survival of
The *'ohana* and the race

Composed by Palani Vaughan

CHAPTER TWO

'Ohana / Family

A Hawaiian man with his Hawaiian-Chinese
wife and their two daughters pose smilingly
for their friend at their Gulick Street home.
Honolulu, circa 1900.
Photographer: Emma D. Richey.
Baker-Van Dyke Collection.

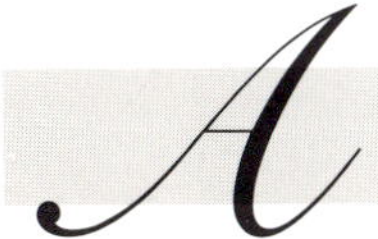

*A*cross the decades, the pride and love of the *'ohana* speaks to us in the family portraits. Gathered on the front steps of their small wooden houses, some with grass-thatched roofs, dressed in their "Sunday best," the Hawaiian generations gaze into the camera, dignified and quiet. A bond of *aloha* is the devotion between parent, child and grandparent. ■ *'Ohana* in Hawaiian means family. The origin of the word is suggested by Andrews to derive from *'ohā,* or the small sprigs of *kalo* or *taro* that grow on the sides of older roots. *Na* is a particle used to add strength to an expression. Thus, the family is like the nurturing plants of the earth, growing upon each other, sharing the subsistence of nature and united in strength. ■ The *makua,* or parent, according to Andrews is the "benefactor or provider" of the *'ohana. Makuakāne* is father and *makuawahine* is mother. The devotion to family was such that the Hawaiians reinforced the structure through the traditional and informal *hānai,* or adoption system. From grandparents to grandchildren, from aunts and uncles to nieces and nephews, the *hānai* system strengthened familial love. Thus *mākua* could refer not only to natural parents, but grandparents and aunts and uncles. ■ The *'ohana* remains a special word to contemporary Hawaiians. From young to old, it is the family that provides nourishment and spirit, laughter and tears and the deepest meaning of being Hawaiian.

Mr. Daniel Ho'olapa, born in 1864, with his wife and grandchildren at his Kahala'u home in North Kona. He is mentioned in Martha Beckwith's *Kumulipo.*
Hilo, Hawai'i, 1925.
Photographer: Theodore Kelsey.
June Gutmanis Collection.

Family in their Sunday best.
'Ula'ino, Maui, 1894.
Photographer: Carl Andrews.
Baker-Van Dyke Collection.

A descendant of chiefs, Curtis Pi'ehu I'aukea (1855–1940) as a baby with his parents, J.W. and Lahapa Nalanipō I'aukea. He was reared in Honolulu by his uncle, Kaihupa'a, an old-time retainer of chiefs and a personal attendant of King Kamehameha III. Curtis went on to become the chamberlain of King Kalākaua and Queen Lili'uokalani. After the over throw of the monarchy, he served both in government and as a trustee of the Lili'uo-kalani Trust and business representative for the former queen. He was one of the most decorated men in Hawai'i. He was married to Charlotte K. Hunks (1877). They had a son and a daughter.
Circa 1856.
Photographer: Unknown.
Baker-Van Dyke Collection.

Right: Mrs. Hulia Kipopa and her family.
Holualoa, Hawai'i, circa 1920–1921.
Photographer: L.R. Sullivan.
Bishop Museum.

Above: Mrs. Louise Kāne and family.
Kohanaiki, Hawai'i, circa 1920–1921.
Photographer: L.R. Sullivan.
Bishop Museum.

A family on the "Forbidden Island"
of Ni'ihau. Note the quilt on the large
grass home.
Ni'ihau, circa ?
Photographer: Francis Sinclair.
Auckland Institute and Museum.

Mrs. William F. Pogue (formerly a Saffrey)
and her children. The mother of Mr. Pogue
(not shown) was a member of the Whitney
missionary family.
Maui, 1910
Photographer: Ray J. Baker.
Baker-Van Dyke Collection.

Mrs. Hea and the John Haili family.
Keʻei, Hawaiʻi, circa 1920–1921.
Photographer: L.R. Sullivan.
Bishop Museum.

James Pōʻahā and family.
Pūkoʻo, Molokaʻi, 1921.
Photographer: L.R. Sullivan.
Bishop Museum.

Mrs. Carrie Luhiau and family.
Hawai'i, circa 1920–1921.
Photographer: L.R. Sullivan.
Bishop Museum.

Left: Charles K. Kamahoahoa and family.
Kohala, Hawai'i, circa 1920–1921.
Photographer: L.R. Sullivan.
Bishop Museum.

Right: Albert Gandall and family.
Līhu'e, Kaua'i, circa 1920–1921.
Photographer: L.R. Sullivan.
Bishop Museum.

Antoine Gasper and family.
Hōnaunau, Hawai'i, circa 1920–1921.
Photographer: L.R. Sullivan.
Bishop Museum.

Robert William Kamakāhi Jr. and family.
Hālawa, Moloka'i, circa 1920–1921.
Photographer: L.R. Sullivan.
Bishop Museum.

Mr. and Mrs. David Kawai with their
niece, Annabel.
Kaululā'au, Lāna'i, 1921.
Photographer: K.P. Emory.
Bishop Museum.

Noa Ka'ōpūiki and friends.
Ka'a, Lāna'i, 1921.
Photographer: K.P. Emory.
Bishop Museum.

Mākua / Parents

Mathaias H. Akona and family.
Kōloa, Kaua'i, circa 1920–1921.
Photographer: L.R. Sullivan.
Bishop Museum.

Left: Dan Mehe'ula and family.
Waimea, Kaua'i, circa 1920–1921.
Photographer: L.R. Sullivan.
Bishop Museum.

John Kealoha Jr. and family.
Keʻei, Hawaiʻi, circa 1920–1921.
Photographer: L.R. Sullivan.
Bishop Museum.

John Maliko Kekua and children.
Pa'uwela, Maui, circa 1920–1921.
Photographer: L.R. Sullivan.
Bishop Museum.

When photographer Ray J. Baker visited the
island of Hawai'i, he often stayed with the
Toomeys. Mr. Samuel K. Toomey was the local
school teacher at Ho'okena. The Toomey
family was well known for their fine singing
voices.
Keālia, Hawai'i, 1916.
Photographer: Ray J. Baker.
Baker-Van Dyke Collection.

John Haili and his son, John Jr.
Keʻei, Hawaiʻi, circa 1920–1921.
Photographer: L.R. Sullivan.
Bishop Museum.

Mrs. Mileka Kala'au and children.
Hālawa, Moloka'i, circa 1920–1921.
Photographer: L.R. Sullivan.
Bishop Museum.

Mr. and Mrs. William Maertens with their
daughter, Anna.
Nāpō'opo'o, Hawai'i, circa 1920–1921.
Photographer: L.R. Sullivan.
Bishop Museum.

Kiaania (1819–1922) of Honoliʻi at Moku-ola
Island, Hilo.
Hilo, Hawaiʻi, circa 1920.
Photographer: Theodore Kelsey.
June Gutmanis Collection.

Kūpuna / Elders

The dark, brown faces of the Hawaiian *kūpuna*, or elders, reflect a wisdom gained through life. The gentle demeanor of Grandmother's face embraces her Polynesian spirit of unselfish, maternal devotion. The long, white beard and deep lines of Grandfather's face gussets a rich lore of storytelling and "know-how" born from experience. The elders are the bearers of love and knowledge, a bridge with the past who help guide the new generations to the future.

The origin of the word *kupuna* is both ancient and diverse. The first root word might be *kupu*, which according to Andrews means "one whose ancestors were born where he himself (or she, herself) was born and vice versa." Combined with *na* which is a particle adding strength to an expression, *kupu* and *na* imply the forefather or ancestor concept of one whose native roots run deep.

In another sense, *kupuna* can be separated into *ku* and *puna*. Andrews defines one of the several meanings of *ku* as "to raise up; to propagate" and defines *puna* as "belonging to a water spring." It is suggested then, that *kūpuna* might be interpreted as "waters that propagate; waters of increase."

The close bond between the *kūpuna* and the future generations is seen in the origins of the word for grandchildren, or *moʻopuna*. Andrews suggests the root word origins *moʻo* and *puna*. *Moʻo* means succession, and *puna*, "springing up as water." *Moʻopuna*, therefore, implies a reference to succeeding generations, as in grandchildren.

One of the more familiar terms used by grandchildren to their elders is *tūtū* or *kūkū*. *Tūtūkāne* refers to grandfather and *tūtūwahine*

to grandmother. These terms are sometimes used to address a grand-uncle or a grand-aunt. Since *tūtū* does not appear in known ancient chants or legends and is not defined by Andrews' early dictionary, the term is probably of recent origin and usage. The traditional *kūpuna*, sometimes shortened to *puna*, or *kupuna kāne* and *kupuna wahine* were considered respectful terms of address.

However they are addressed, the *kūpuna* and the children have retained a strong bond in Hawaiian ways. The *hānai*, or adoption system, has enriched that relationship as *kūpuna* and *moʻopuna* are considered like parent and child. The little ones give to the elders their laughter and joy for a new life. And the *kūpuna* pass on the knowledge and lore of the old Hawaiian traditions. The *moʻopuna*, waters of succession, follow the flow of the *kūpuna*, waters of propagation.

Judge and scholar John Papa 'Ī'ī
(1800?–1870), the son of a Kona chief,
was born at Waipi'o, 'Ewa, O'ahu. He joined
the royal court at the age of ten, where he
became the companion of the future
Kamehameha II. He took the name of "Papa"
from his uncle, and the name of "'Ī'ī" from an
exclamation by Prince Liholiho when he first
saw his future friend.

He had a distinguished public career.
He helped the missionaries in the transla-
tion of texts into Hawaiian. Articles by him
appearing in the newspaper *Kū'oko'a* from
1866 to 1870 were collected and translated
as valuable contributions to Hawaiiana; see
Fragments of Hawaiian History.
Honolulu, 1867.
Photographer: H.L. Chase.
Baker-Van Dyke Collection.

A venerable Hawaiian woman wearing a lei
niho palaoa and holding a hand kāhili.
Circa 1895.
Photographer: Unknown.
Bishop Museum.

Mrs. William Ka'imieka.
Kamuela, Hawai'i, circa 1920–1921.
Photographer: L.R. Sullivan.
Bishop Museum.

S.W. Kī'uo. An elderly face, exquisitely
modeled with the lines of advancing years,
yet filled with calmness, tranquility and
serenity.
Nāpō'opo'o, Hawai'i, circa 1920–1921.
Photographer: L.R. Sullivan.
Bishop Museum.

On the way to Alakea Street wharf to sell
lauhala fans, mats and hats to incoming
passengers on "boat day."
Honolulu, 1899.
Photographer: Emma D. Richey.
Baker-Van Dyke Collection.

A resident of Lunalilo Home—a splendid face, furnishing in silent eloquence, a vision of the past.
Honolulu, circa 1900–1910.
Photographer: Alonzo Gartley.
Bishop Museum.

Mrs. Kūhiō from Waiakea
Circa ?
Photographer: Theodore Kelsey.
June Gutmanis Collection.

Right: Ka'uhane Kukololua
Kahe'a, Lāna'i, 1921.
Photographer: K.P. Emory.
Bishop Museum.

Right: Mrs. Wilmot Vredenburg and her
grandson, Wilmot.
Kamuela, Hawai'i, circa 1920–1921.
Photographer: L.R. Sullivan.
Bishop Museum.

Joseph H. Kī'aha.
Kohanaiki, Hawai'i, circa 1920–1921.
Photographer: L.R. Sullivan.
Bishop Museum.

Two generations share a moment together.
Hōnaunau, Hawai'i, circa 1900–1912.
Photographer: Alonzo Gartley.
Bishop Museum.

Ka'uhane 'Āpiki and his wife, Ho'ohuli.
Lāna'i, 1921.
Photographer: K.P. Emory.
Bishop Museum.

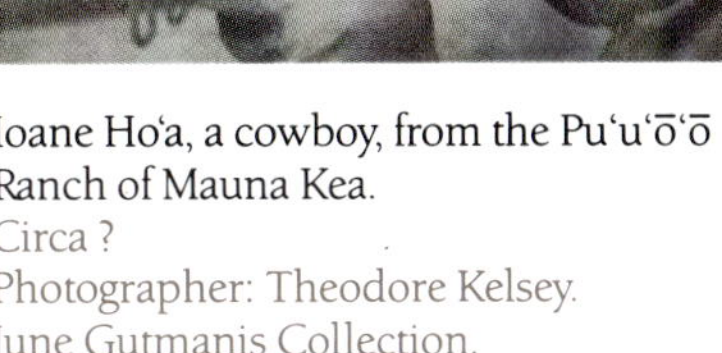

Left: Pa'alani, from the Pu'ueo side of the mouth of the Wailuku River. He was known for his knowledge of chants and stones.
Hilo, Hawai'i, circa ?
Photographer: Theodore Kelsey.
June Gutmanis Collection.

Ioane Ho'a, a cowboy, from the Pu'u'ō'ō Ranch of Mauna Kea.
Circa ?
Photographer: Theodore Kelsey.
June Gutmanis Collection.

Mr. and Mrs. John T. Kīko'o with their granddaughter.
Honolulu, 1918.
Photographer: Ray J. Baker.
Baker-Van Dyke Collection.

A coffee planter and his donkey. The donkeys were referred to by all as "Kona nightingales."
Kailua-Kona, Hawai'i, 1908.
Photographer: Ray J. Baker.
Baker-Van Dyke Collection.

Keiki / Children

Children of this land before. . .
> At play on golden sands
> Of these blue Pacific shores

Children of this land before. . .
> Walked upon their Polynesian
> land of ancient Hawaiian lore

Children of this land before. . .
> The *kama*, the *lei*,
> the *pua*, the *liko*
> Were *keiki o ka ʻāina*

Children of the Hawaiian People

Composed by Palani Vaughan

The laughter of *keiki*, a child or offspring, is precious to the Hawaiian. Like the flowering bud of a plant, a child is a delicate, beautiful creation that moves with joy, curiosity and innocence through a world of discovery.

Keiki, according to Andrews, is a combination of the article *ke*, which means "the," and *iki*, which is "little or small," producing *ke iki*, or "the little one." Over time, *ke iki* came to be treated as one word and subsequently required the use of an additional article in speech, resulting in *ke keiki*, or "the child," and *na keiki*, or "the children."

The Hawaiian's love for their children is expressed through and symbolized by the poetic terms of endearment used in connection with children—*lei, pua* and *liko*, which translate respectively to "wreath, flower and flower bud."

Children who were favored by parents, grandparents, uncles and aunts were called *punahele* or *kamalani*. Pūkuʻi-Elbert defines *punahele* as "a favorite; to treat as a favorite." It was said that *kūpuna*, or grandparents, often carried petted children on their shoulders. Thus, *puna*, which is the shortened version for *kupuna*, combined with *hele*, which Pūkuʻi-Elbert defines as "to go; to move," conveys the image of pampering Hawaiian grandparents carrying the object of their affections about on their shoulders.

Kama is listed by Andrews as another term for child and *lani* for chief. Thus *kamalani* was "the child of a chief" or "a favorite or petted child." Pūkuʻi-Elbert adds that the figurative meaning of *kamalani* is "finicky, fussy," an interpretation that was probably a result of the indulgence with which that favored child was treated.

When *kama* is combined with *liʻi*, which Pūkuʻi-Elbert defines as meaning "small," the resulting word is *kamaliʻi*, or "small child," a term generally applied to children.

In the last century, when the alarming high death rate of the Hawaiian people had reduced the native population to a low of 44,000, the fragileness of children was of special concern. King Kalākaua extolled his people to *hoʻoulu lāhui*, "to increase the nation." A flourishing population of *keiki* was seen as the last hope of Hawaiʻi, as the seeds of racial survival. Their laughter, fortunately, was not extinguished and one hundred years later, the children still bring joy to the Hawaiian Islands.

Left: Hawaiian girl, possibly at the Paul Kelsom residence in Piʻihonua. Circa ? Photographer: Theodore Kelsey. June Gutmanis Collection.

Hawai'i's early photographers were
captivated by the sight of Hawaiian children,
often without any clothes, playing on the
beaches with complete abandoment.
Maui, 1912.
Photographer: Ray J. Baker.
Bishop Museum.

Above: Four girls on Kūhiō Beach, near Prince
Kūhiō's residence. In the left background,
a pier extends from the Peacock home, the
future 1900 site of the Moana Hotel.
Waikīkī, circa 1890s.
Photographer: Alonzo Gartley.
Bishop Museum.

A future beauty shows her best smile. The
shadow indicates late afternoon and perhaps
she is getting hungry.
Kona, Hawai'i, 1912.
Photographer: Ray J. Baker.
Baker-Van Dyke Collection.

Fishing for ʻōpae (shrimp) in a fishpond at
Hakipuʻu, near Kualoa.
Oʻahu, 1914.
Photographer: Ray J. Baker.
Baker-Van Dyke Collection.

Above: Children in front of the double canoe
that brought Queen Liliʻuokalani ashore in
Hilo during her May 1891 tour.
Hilo, Hawaiʻi, 1891.
Photographer: Unknown.
Bishop Museum.

Enjoying the beach.
Lāhainā, Maui, 1908.
Photographer: Ray J. Baker.
Bishop Museum.

At the beach landing near Hoʻokena.
Hoʻokena, Hawaiʻi, circa 1888.
Photographer: J.A. Gonsalves.
Baker-Van Dyke Collection.

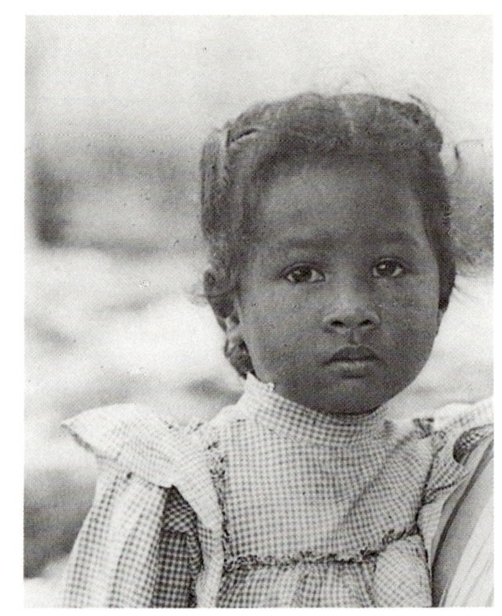

A shy girl on her mule. She eventually smiled.
Kohala, Hawai'i, 1912.
Photographer: Ray J. Baker.
Bishop Museum.

Left: Hawaiian girl.
Circa 1910.
Photographer: Alonzo Gartley.
Bishop Museum.

Two Hawaiian boys with glistening
bronze bodies.
Circa 1905–1915.
Photographer: Chock Chong.
Bishop Museum.

A group of Hawaiian children. The oldest
appears unhappy perhaps because of the
responsibility of caring for her sisters.
Circa 1890.
Photographer: Unknown.
Bishop Museum.

Group of young boys.
Hilo, Hawai'i, circa ?
Photographer: Unknown.
Bishop Museum.

Above: Boys standing on a pier contemplating
"boat day," when they will be able to dive
for money.
Honolulu, circa ?
Photographer: Unknown.
Bishop Museum.

Two young Hawaiian boys, one obviously
wishing to be unidentifiable.
Circa 1910.
Photographer: Unknown.
Bishop Museum.

Hawaiian girl.
Circa 1900.
Photographer: Unknown.
Bishop Museum.

A backyard performance.
Circa 1920.
Photographer: Unknown.
Bishop Museum.

Hula girl.
Circa 1920.
Photographer: J. J. Williams.
Baker-Van Dyke Collection.

Hawaiian girl.
Circa 1900.
Photographer: F. Davey.
Bishop Museum.

Waimea School children.
Waimea, Hawai'i, circa 1920–1921.
Photographer: L.R. Sullivan.
Bishop Museum.

KawaiaHa'o seminary students on King Street
near the present site of City Hall.
Honolulu, Circa ?
Photographer: Unknown.
Hawaiian Mission Children's Society.

Graduating classes of The Kamehameha
School for Boys and The Kamehameha
School for Girls.
Honolulu, circa 1906.
Photographer: Rice and Perkins.
Baker-Van Dyke Collection.

Powerful god of the ancient
Hawaiian people.
ʻŌʻō-wielding *Kāne,*
Who gave sacred life-giving water
to the land.

Proud Hawaiian man
and husband,
Dignified in stature and maturity,
Possessed of the life-giving water.

Hawaiian woman and loving wife
Of *kāne,* the man-husband,
Gives powerful meaning to
the life-giving water of man.

Composed by Palani Vaughan

Margaret K. Martin (Mrs. Henry G.
Bertleman).
Honolulu, 1895.
Photographer: J.J. Williams.
Baker-Van Dyke Collection.

A captain of an inter-island steamer.
Honolulu, 1890.
Photographer: J.J. Williams.
Baker-Van Dyke Collection.

In the life of a man and a woman are many cycles which the Hawaiians recognized with distinct names. When the *keiki*, or child, became a teenager, he was called *'ōpio*, or *na po'e 'ōpio*, young people. *'Ōpio* or *'ōpiopio*, is defined by Andrews as "young: juvenile, as a person" or "young, as a person or animal; immature." Andrews adds that *'ōpiopio* also means "junior; son of a father of the same name."

Na po'e 'ōpio matured into the next stage of human development called *u'i*, defined by Pūku'i-Elbert as people of "youthful vigor and beauty." They are in a period of life call *ka wā u'i*, "the age of youthful vigor grace and beauty; the age of greatest physical beauty." Pūku'i-Elbert adds that they are *na po'e u'i*, "young people, as in the late teens and early twenties." This period of life in today's world is usually considered a difficult one, during which disrespect, antagonism and defiance become a mark of "growing up." The Hawaiians of old, recognizing the need for positive support during this cycle of life, thus conveyed to the young people an admiration for youthful vigor and great physical beauty by referring to them as *u'i*. This encouragement and loving support during a period of trouble was a profound insight that could have important modern applications.

When *na po'e u'i* attained full maturity, each one had reached *kanaka makua*, which, according to Andrews, is "a state of mature age whether one has children or not." Pūku'i-Elbert explains that *kanaka makua* means "to become adult, or to obtain the strength and maturity of an adult."

Kāne is the term used for "adult man" or to designate the male gender, but Pūku'i-Elbert expands the definition to include "husband, male sweetheart, man," and states that "it is the name of one of the four leading gods." *Wahine* is the term used for "woman," and according to Pūku'i-Elbert, it also means "lady, wife; womanliness, female, femininity; feminine."

In marriage, men and women of old Hawai'i held positive views of themselves and their relationships. Man, or husband, shared the name of a powerful god called *Kāne*, and woman, or wife, who lovingly served her *kāne* was as reflected in an old adage related by Andrews:

> *Wahine, he mea ia e nani ai*
> *ke kāne,*
> *He lei ali'i maika'i no ke kāne.*
> Woman, she gives honor
> to the man,
> She is a crown of beauty for
> the husband.

Since the *hānai* adoption system frequently resulted in the rearing of children by the *kūpuna*, the *kāne* and *wahine* were able to devote themselves to the full development of their prowess and physical beauty. In work, sport, dance or intellect, adult life was devoted to attaining an excellence in skill and accomplishments. In the final cycle of life, when *kāne* and *wahine* became aged *'elemakule* and *luahine*, they could reflect back with dignity on a life that was marked with the full enjoyment of human activity, joy, knowledge and prayer. The photographs of the men and women of old Hawai'i attest to the fullness and dignity of the lives they lived in their island home.

David Malo (1793?–1853) was brought up in the household of the high chief Kuakini (John Adams), brother of Kaʻahumanu. Then, having become a Christian, he lived with the Rev. William Richards at Lāhainā, Maui. In his late thirties, he entered the first class at Lahainaluna Seminary. He had learned to read and write in the Hawaiian language, and helped Richards in his translations of part of the Bible. Ordained as a minister, Malo in his later years was pastor of the Congregational Church at Kalepolepo, Maui.

Around 1840, he wrote down many chants, genealogies and other Hawaiian traditions which were translated in 1903 by N. B. Emerson as *Hawaiian Antiquities*. Drawing by A.T. Agate of the United States Exploring Expedition.
Van Dyke Collection.

Left: Two men at the Makaokūikalani Stone.
Hawaiian men were noted for their strength
and robust appearance.
Circa ?
Photographer: Theodore Kelsey.
Bishop Museum.

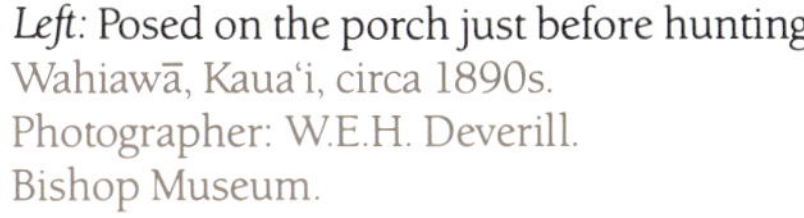

Left: Posed on the porch just before hunting.
Wahiawā, Kaua'i, circa 1890s.
Photographer: W.E.H. Deverill.
Bishop Museum.

David Ka'apu of Punalu'u.
O'ahu, 1932.
Photographer: Ray J. Baker.
Baker-Van Dyke Collection.

The famous Kahanamoku brothers
from L. to R.: Bill, Sam, Louis,
David, Sargent, Duke.
Waikīkī, circa 1928.
Photographer: Tai Sing Loo.
Bishop Museum.

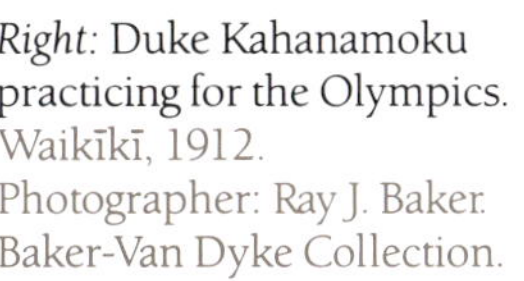

Right: Duke Kahanamoku
practicing for the Olympics.
Waikīkī, 1912.
Photographer: Ray J. Baker.
Baker-Van Dyke Collection.

Olympic swimmer Duke
Kahanamoku.
Waikīkī, 1916.
Photographer: Ray J. Baker.
Baker-Van Dyke Collection.

DUKE KAHANAMOKU

*Duke Kahanamoku (1890–1968)
was born in Haleakalā, Maui, son of
Duke Halapu Kahanamoku and Julia
Paoakania Lonokahini Kahanamoku. As
a youth he became a master surfer on a
sixteen-foot koa-wood board weighing
114 pounds. In 1910, he developed what
he called "the Hawaiian crawl," a basic
swimming competition stroke today
known as "the American crawl."*
■ *Kahanamoku won an AAU meet
in Honolulu Harbor, breaking United
States records for the 100- and 50-yard
sprints. He went to the Stockholm
Olympics in 1912 and swept the swimming events, setting a world record for
the 100-meter event; in the same year
he broke his own record at Hamburg.*
■ *He entered competition again in
1916 and broke more records with his
distinctive style. At almost thirty years of
age, he beat his own 100-meter freestyle
record at the Antwerp Olympics in 1920
by making the course in one minute flat.
He lost his title in the 1924 Olympics in
Paris to Johnny Weissmuller. Kahanamoku became a national hero when, on
June 14, 1925, he rescued on his surf-
board eight of the twelve men saved from
a capsized fishing boat in high surf off
Newport Beach, California. He won
medals in the 1928 Olympics.* ■ *In
1932, won a spot on the United States
water-polo team and thus appeared in
four Olympic competitions in twenty
years.* ■ *(from A. Grove Day, "History
Makers of Hawaii")*

Naʻauao Kaʻōpūiki, Abraham
Kauila and ʻInokā Makahanaloa.
Keōmuku, Lānaʻi, 1921.
Photographer: K.P. Emory.
Bishop Museum.

Resting under a tree, a time-out
from a hard day's work of hunting.
Circa 1920s.
Photographer: Theodore Kelsey.
Bishop Museum.

Right: Lameka Ahu-lau of Wailuku,
Puhonua, who lived at Waiānuenue below
the Hilo Hospital.
Circa ?
Photographer: Theodore Kelsey.
June Gutmanis Collection.

James Kauila.
Keōmuku, Lāna'i, 1921.
Photographer: K.P. Emory.
Bishop Museum.

Oliver Kaniau.
Kailua, Hawai'i, circa 1920–1921.
Photographer: L.R. Sullivan.
Bishop Museum.

Kaliko Makakoa.
Maui, circa 1920–1921.
Photographer: L.R. Sullivan.
Bishop Museum.

The second watch—Honolulu
policemen, on August 6, 1911.
Honolulu, 1911.
Photographer: L.E. Edgeworth.
Bishop Museum.

Hawaiian woman.
Circa 1870s.
Photographer: A.A. Montano.
Baker-Van Dyke Collection.

Emma Alexandria Kalanikauika'alaneo
Kiliaulaninuiamamao Defries, born on Strong
Island, January 20, 1856, the daughter of Rev.
M. Kānoa, a missionary from Hawai'i to the
Gilbert Islands.
Honolulu, 1895.
Photographer: J.J. Williams
Baker-Van Dyke Collection.

Hawaiian woman.
Circa 1870s.
Photographer: A.A. Montano.
Baker-Van Dyke Collection.

Hawaiian woman.
Circa 1876–1885.
Photographer: A.A. Montano.
Baker-Van Dyke Collection.

A studio portrait.
Circa 1870–1882.
Photographer: M. Dickson.
Bishop Museum.

Hawaiian women enjoyed formal dresses.
This charming lady was no exception.
Circa ?
Photographer: unknown.
Bishop Museum.

Women in party dresses. They were probably
friends or neighbors of the photographer,
who visited Hawai'i in 1886 and 1892.
Circa 1890.
Photographer: Alfred Mitchell
Bishop Museum.

Hawaiian woman wearing leis.
Circa ?
Photographer: Theodore Kelsey.
June Gutmanis Collection.

Right: Young Hilo beauty.
Circa ?
Photographer: Theodore Kelsey.
June Gutmanis Collection.

Five ladies, possibly retainers of King
Kalākaua. Top row from L to R: Kalua,
Kapehekawelo, Victoria ʻIkuwā. Bottom
row from L to R: Kalua-Ahi Nu, Haliʻilehua.
Circa 1890s.
Photographer: J.J. Williams.
Bishop Museum.

Ambrotype of Hawaiian women.
Circa 1856.
Photographer: Unknown.
Bishop Museum.

Graduation picture.
Honolulu, circa 1900.
Photographer: Rice and Perkins
Hawai‘i State Archives

Facing page: A well-to-do lady dressed in the latest fashions of her time.
Circa 1876–1885.
Photographer: A.A. Montano.
Bishop Museum.

Preceding page:
In a rural setting, at an age when life is carefree, these young ladies let their hair down.
Circa 1890s.
Photographer: A. Mitchell.
Hawai'i State Archives.

Above: Madame Alapa'i, famed singer of the Royal Hawaiian Band, with a friend after a concert.
Honolulu, 1908.
Photographer: Emma D. Richey.
Baker-Van Dyke Collection.

A stately lei seller at Alakea Street wharf.
Honolulu, 1912.
Photographer: Ray J. Baker.
Baker-Van Dyke Collection.

Kūkona, (Mrs. John Porter) of Hilo, with her
daughter, Mrs. Conradt.
Hilo, Hawai'i, circa ?
Photographer: Theodore Kelsey.
June Gutmanis Collection.

Moloka'i women on an excursion.
Moloka'i, 1924.
Photographer: Ray J. Baker.
Bishop Museum.

Right: Hawaiian woman.
Circa 1895.
Photographer: J.J. Williams.
Hawai'i State Archives.

Pāʻū rider.
Circa ?
Photographer: Tai Sing Loo.
Bishop Museum.

Hawaiian woman.
Circa ?
Photographer: Theodore Kelsey.
June Gutmanis Collection.

Relaxing on a mat.
Circa 1900–1912.
Photographer: Alonzo Gartley.
Bishop Museum.

Mrs. Mary Fitzsimmons, a teacher at
Keōmuku School.
Lāna'i, 1921.
Photographer: K.P. Emory.
Bishop Museum.

With mokihana berry leis.
Kaua'i, circa 1900's.
Photographer: Mabel Putnam Chilson.
Bishop Museum.

KŪLANAKAUHALE
Ancient village
of Hawaiians of old.
Seaside fishing village of
ocean calm and plenty,
Where brave village men,
Lawaiʻa, fished the deep sea,
And where village women
and children,
Lawaiʻa kōkō, fished the teeming
shallow ocean reefs.

KŪLANAKAUHALE
Ancient Hawaiian rural village
of country-dwelling people of old,
Who farmed the *ʻāina*
as well as the sea.
Village where rugged
mahiʻai farmers,
With determination,
cultivated the soil
Using the ancient
ʻōʻō digging staff,
Bringing added sustenance
to the village.

Composed by Palani Vaughan

CHAPTER THREE

Kūlanakauhale / Village Life

Activity in the water—fishing, paddling,
playing. To the Hawaiians, the ocean was
everything: food, sport, recreation and
transportation.
Ni'ihau, circa ?
Photographer: Francis Sinclair.
Auckland Institute and Museum.

Right: Ready to go surfing. The structure was
probably a temporary dwelling to provide
comfort and protection from the sun while
the family was at the beach.
Circa 1890s.
Photographer: Severin.
Bishop Museum.

here exists an old Hawai'i found today only in the more remote mountain and seaside regions. It is a Hawai'i of families bonded together in work, pleasure and prayer—of lifestyles and values shaped by nature, spirit and love. The images of village life that speak to us in century-old, faded photographs invite us to step into that other world where Hawaiian life found its richest and most endearing expression. ■ One of the Hawaiian words used by Pūku'i-Elbert to define "village" is *kūlanakauhale. Kūlana* means a "place, site or situation," and *kauhale* defined as a "group of houses comprising a Hawaiian home." The literal definition of *kūlanakauhale* is therefore "situation plural house." ■ A closer examination of the root words gives greater insight to the meaning of *kūlanakauhale. Ku* is defined by Pūku'i-Elbert as "to stand, stop, anchor; to stay, remain." *Lana* means "moored; to lie at anchor, as a fishing canoe." *Kau* is a particle indicating plurality and *hale* is "house, building." Therefore, *kūlanakauhale* is a term that could be interpreted as an ideal setting for a thriving seaside village, possessing calm, offshore reef waters, suitable for fishing or for anchoring or beaching canoes. ■ Fishing was, after all, an important enterprise for any Hawaiian seaside village because the sea provided the food that sustained human life. *I'a,* or fish of many kinds, *'ōpae-kai,* shrimp; *he'e,* octopus or squid; *mūhe'e,* cuttlefish; *honu,* sea-turtle; *loli,* sea-cucumber; *'opihi* and other varieties of shell fish; sea urchins such as *wana; pāpa'i,* crabs of many kinds and other crustacea; and *limu,* seaweed of several varieties, gave sustenance to the fishing village. ■ Those who fished the ocean were called *lawai'a,* a work activity exclusive to the males. Inshore reef fishing with fine mesh nets, *lawai'a kōkō,* was performed by the women and children. Pūku'i-Elbert defines *lawai'a* as "to fish" and *kōkō* as a "carrying net." ■ Sometimes geographic conditions were so ideal that *kō'ele,* ocean fishponds, were created for fish farming purposes by villagers on behalf of the landholding chief or king. The fishponds could hold hundreds of thriving, reproductive fish in support of villages with large resident populations. ■ Fishing village residents wouldn't necessarily engage in agricultural pursuits if geographic limitations prevented successful farming. In such cases, the villagers bartered for any needed agricultural products with inland villages where farming was possible. Land was cultivated in these areas for the chiefs or king, planting wetland or dryland, *kalo* or *taro; 'uala,* sweet potatoes; *mai'a,* cooking bananas; *'ulu,* breadfruit; coconut and other foods. ■ Farmers were called *mahi'ai.* Andrews explains that the word is derived from two root words, *mahi* which means "to dig the ground for the purpose of planting food" and *'ai,* which means "food." *Mahi'ai* used a digging stick for tilling the soil called *'ō'ō.* ■ Through agriculture, villagers also successfully cultivated small *wauke,* mulberry trees, the bark of which was mallet-beaten into a paper cloth called *kapa.* The *kapa* was colored or dye-stamped and used for clothing and bed-

Fisherwoman with her net ready to catch
shrimp in tidewater pools.
Circa 1890s.
Photographer: Unknown.
Baker-Van Dyke Collection.

Preparing ʻauhuhu, a fish poisoning plant.
Honaunau, Hawaiʻi, circa 1920.
Photographer: John F. Stokes.
Bishop Museum.

ding. ■ Agriculture for the king existed even after the 1848 Great Māhele, or
land division, initiated by King Kamehameha III. Under the Great Māhele, the
people received from the king fee simple title to specific plots of land, or ʻāpana,
within their respective villages. Certain land parcels were designated as planta-
tions for the king and were called *Kōʻele* like the king's fishponds, or sometimes
referred to as *Pōʻalima*, both terms meaning "Friday." The designation was appropriate since the people were required to work the king's land every Friday.
■ Rural village life was not an easy existence. It required sturdy, industrious and
dedicated people, capable of sustaining their families and themselves with provi-
sions from the sea and the land. Yet, it was a lifestyle that intertwined the people
to the beauty of the earth, water, air, wind, mist, rain, sun and fire. The *kūlanakauhale* was a simpler way of life in which the rewards of harmony, love and inter-
dependency were immediate and ineffable. To gaze back into the villages of old Hawaiʻi is to be reminded of how much is lost
in the pursuit of progress.

Kawika Shintani (little boy) and John Ku'ualoha Ka'ohelauli'i ride across a freshwater pond. Such large ponds would disappear during summer.
Ni'ihau, circa 1923.
Photographer: Unknown.
Bishop Museum.

Left: Net throwing. In old Hawai'i, fishing was one of the most highly specialized occupations. It required much training and began at sunrise. Fishermen invoked not only their skills and techniques as craftsmen but the supernatural as well. Religion and fishing were closely related and the fishing gods were never neglected.
Pūko'o, Moloka'i, 1912.
Photographer: Ray J. Baker.
Baker-Van Dyke Collection.

Fishing scene. Hukilau in progress.
Circa 1900–1912.
Photographer: Alonzo Gartley.
Bishop Museum.

Relaxing on the porch late in the day after a
hard day's toil in the fields and patches.
Circa 1900–1912.
Photographer: Alonzo Gartley.
Bishop Museum.

Drying fish on the beach.
Ho'okena, Hawai'i, 1927.
Photographer: Ray J. Baker.
Baker-Van Dyke Collection.

Right: The location of villages was
determined by the proximity of agricultural
land, the availability of fresh water, and the
closeness of seashore with prolific fishing
grounds (or surf sites). Houses were kept tidy
and clean, although they were not positioned
in any apparent order. In these photographs
there are contrasts between the "old" and
the new. Grass houses are amid wooden
dwellings; on the right, the frame of a grass
house under construction. It is "steamer day"
and the whole town has turned out for the
arrival of the boat.
Near Ho'okena, South Kona, Hawai'i, 1888.
Photographer: J.A. Gonsalves.
Baker-Van Dyke Collection.

Eating poi.
Lāhainā, Maui, 1901.
Photographer: Emma D. Richey.
Baker-Van Dyke Collection.

A man and his worldly possessions—a trunk
filled with memories.
Circa 1900.
Photographer: Unknown (possibly
Theodore Kelsey).
Bishop Museum.

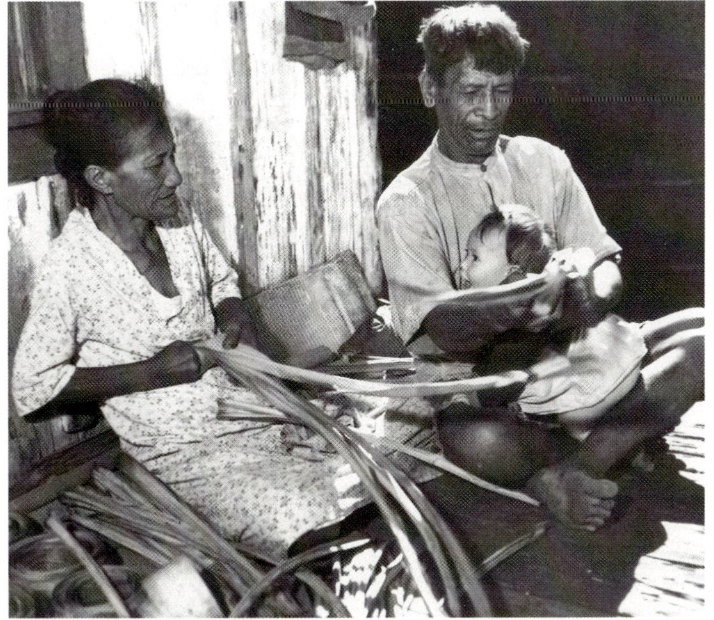

A family rolls and strips lauhala for weaving.
The child obviously enjoys the comfort of her
grandfather's lap.
Pohoiki, Puna, Hawai'i, 1932.
Photographer: Ray J. Baker.
Baker-Van Dyke Collection.

Family gathered on the porch.
Circa 1918.
Photographer: Theodore Kelsey.
Bishop Museum.

Living on the edge of a pineapple field.
Papayas are in the hanging basket.
Circa 1915.
Photographer: Ray J. Baker.
Baker-Van Dyke Collection.

Rural lifestyle.
Kailua-Kona, Hawai'i, 1910
Photographer: Ray J. Baker.
Baker-Van Dyke Collection.

David Kaʻiwa Jr. and David Kaʻiwa Sr. maintain the family treasures.
Photographer: Ray J. Baker.
Baker-Van Dyke Collection.

Poi was prepared by peeling the cooked taro roots with a shell or a stone knife and then pounding it to a paste upon special boards of ʻōhiʻa or koa. The patterned pounders are two distinct models, but usually the collar button type was preferred. In the foreground are three gourds—vessels that are very rare today.
Circa ?
Photographer: Unknown.
Hawaiian Mission Children's Society.

In front of the family home.
Circa 1890.
Photographer: W.E.H. Deverrill
Bishop Museum.

A contrast of the old and new: grass
structures beside wooden homes. Types of
grass houses varied according to the location
and availability of materials.
Ni'ihau, circa ?
Photographer: Francis Sinclair.
Auckland Institute and Museum.

Left: At his Waiākea homestead, Phillip
Luahiwa, an old hula expert from Hanalei,
Kaua'i. He also lived near Hilo, in Honolulu
near Lēʻahi hospital, and finally at Honapu,
Hawai'i. It was not unusual for Hawaiian men
and women advanced in years to still work
a full day.
Circa ?
Photographer: Theodore Kelsey.
June Gutmanis Collection.

Hui / Gatherings

A special outing in the country.
ʻĪao Valley, Maui, circa 1880s.
Photographer: H.L. Chase.
Bishop Museum.

erriment, pride and the spirit of *aloha* flow through a Hawaiian gathering. The children scurry about with handfuls of *haupia*, squealing in play and mischief, or silently listening to the adults who "talk story." Elsewhere, an impromptu song and dance erupts as young people join in the excitement of the music. The old folks are tending the babies and sharing memories and everyone is partaking in the feast of Hawaiian food and drink. ■ The gatherings are of many kinds in the Hawaiian community. Some are joyous; others are solemn and respectful. Some are rich with sport, dance and feasting; others are dignified pageants of traditional importance. All of the gatherings, from backyard *lūʻau* to statewide celebrations, are the communal bonds that continually give pride to being Hawaiian.

Lū'au gathering.
Hōnaunau, Hawai'i, circa 1900–1910.
Photographer: Alonzo Gartley.
Bishop Museum.

Large gathering including some non-
Hawaiians for a lū‘au.
Circa pre-1900.
Photographer: Unknown.
Bishop Museum.

Delegates from Hawaiian churches from
all the islands at the annual meeting of the
Hawaiian Evangelical Association.
Honolulu, 1934.
Photographer: Ray J. Baker.
Baker-Van Dyke Collection.

A hoʻokupu (offering) to Governor Pinkham
from the homesteaders of Makiki Heights.
Circa 1913–1918.
Photographer: Unknown.
Bishop Museum.

Left: A large gathering for a lūʻau or picnic.
Circa 1900.
Photographer: Unknown.
Bishop Museum.

'Ahahui / Hawaiian Societies

Ancient sennit of strength
of binding strength,
Holding firm in lashing storms
The sacred canoes of the
people of old.

'AHA

Ancient prayer of taboo
and power.
Binding *kapu*,
Holding firm against all danger
The ancient kingdom.

'AHAHUI

Society of Hawaiian people,
Unified by the binding cord
of tradition and proud heritage,
Standing firm with dignity against
storms of change.

Composed by Palani Vaughan

Left: Princess Elizabeth Kahanu Kalaniana'ole in front of the Kamehameha statue on Kamehameha Day.
Honolulu, 1919.
Photographer: Unknown.
Bishop Museum.

One type of formal gathering which has become extremely important to contemporary Hawaiians is the *'ahahui*, which Pūku'i-Elbert defines as a "society, club, association" of various types. The root words reveal a combination of two concepts: *'aha* and *hui*. Andrews defines *'aha* as a "company or assembly of people for any purpose." However, Andrews also states that *'aha* is "a cord braided from the husk of the coconut" and originated "in the fact that coconut fiber is very strong when braided into strings." Andrews remarks further that *'aha* was "the name of a certain prayer connected with a *kapu* or taboo."

Therefore, this prayer with its *kapu* was likened to the strongly braided coconut fiber sennit which could strengthen a canoe in a storm. The prayer, explains Andrews, "was supposed to be very efficacious in holding the kingdom together in times of danger." *Hui* means "to assemble together, as people for business." Similarly, Pūku'i-Elbert defines *hui* as "to form a society or organization; to meet." Therefore, it can be inferred that *'ahahui* is an assemblage of people who have convened for a purpose and who are united by, perhaps, a charter or constitution which gives the collective body organizational strength in order to maintain its survival.

The variety of formal *'ahahui* in modern Hawai'i are quite numerous, ranging from genealogical societies such as the 'Ahahui Māmakakaua, Ka'ahumanu Society, Order of Kamehameha or Hale of Nāli'i, to the diverse Hawaiian civic clubs.

One dignified *'ahahui* of particular note orginated in the last century. Its membership is derived from the ranks of Hawaiian families who can substatiate ancestral descent from ancient chiefly Hawaiian warriors.

Although *'ahahui* existed during late monarchial times, it went "underground" approximately during the reign of King Kalākaua. The *'ahahui* remained a clandestine organization through the years that Hawai'i was a Provisional Government and a Republic. It continued to meet secretly, even after Hawai'i became a territory of the United States.

The *'ahahui* finally resurfaced in 1912 to formally incorporate as a genealogical society on October 30, 1917. Today it is called The Daughters And Sons of Hawaiian Warriors, or sometimes by its Hawaiian name, *'Ahahui Māmakakaua. Māmakakaua* means "company of warriors," according to Pūku'i-Elbert, or is literally translated as "carriers of war."

The organization is led by a female *Kuhina Nui* or "Premier," as it has been for most of its existence. For the past 31 years, Mrs. Healani Doane, a descendant of the Kamehameha *Nui 'ai lū'au* (Chiefly Line), has ably led this proud organization of Hawaiian men and women with calm dignity. Its past members have included such distinguished *ali'i* as Queen Lili'uokalani and Prince Jonah Kūhio, Kalaniana'ole and his wife, Princess Kahanu, both of whom served as *Mō'ī* at one time.

Since its revivification in 1912, *'ahahui māmakakaua* has compiled a notable record of dedicated service in representing the Hawaiian community. With dignified tradition, ceremony and chants, society members, wearing impressive and distinctive colored feathered shoulder capes and cloaks, over the years have extended honors to

visiting foreign royalty and other
dignitaries. In 1985, 'Ahahui Māmakakaua received Prince Hitachi, one of
the royal sons of Japan's Emperor
Hirohito, who had come to Hawai'i
to pay royal homage to the memory
of His Majesty King Kalākaua at
the Royal Mausoleum situated at
"Mauna'ala" in Nu'uanu Valley.

In this same notable fashion
and in the noble manner of their
ancient royal ancestors, the 'Ahahui
Māmakakaua is most often seen in
public appearances today when
paying homage to the memories of
past royal Hawaiian ali'i and former
kings and queens of Hawai'i, such as
King Kamehameha I, King Kalākaua
and Queen Lili'uokalani.

'Ahahui Māmakakaua often
extends invitations to participate in
their ceremonies to other noteworthy
sister and brother Hawaiian societies
with long traditions in Hawai'i. These
respected societies include the Ka'a-
humanu Society (which is the oldest),
Order of Kamehameha, and Hale
O Nāli'i.

The Hawaiian Civic Clubs from
both the continental United States
as well as Hawai'i have also played a

vital role in preserving the Hawaiian
heritage. In November of each year,
these civic clubs along with the
'ahahui societies convene together.

Hawaiian Civic Club formation
was encouraged by Prince Kūhiō
as a means of unifying the Hawaiian
people. Hawaiian societies and civic
clubs definitely have played an
important role in fulfilling the aspira-
tions of Prince Kūhiō. The activities
of these organizations have not only
unified Hawaiians, but have enriched
the lives of their members, the Hawaiian community, and the broader
statewide community, as well.

It is fitting in the Year of the
Hawaiian that recognition and
respect be given to these esteemed
Hawaiian organizations whose
activities throughout the generations
have helped to perpetuate native
Hawaiians' colorful and meaningful
heritage for posterity.

Celebration at Hulihe'e Palace.
Kailua-Kona, Hawai'i, circa 1890.
Photographer: Unknown.
Bishop Museum.

Kamaeokalani Māhoe, acting as Queen
Ka'ahumanu on the Centennial Celebration
of the arrival of the first missionaries, which
ended at the Tableau at Punahou School.
Honolulu, April 1920.
Photographer: Unknown.
Bishop Museum.

A parade celebrating King Kalākaua's 50th
birthday jubilee, King and Fort streets.
Honolulu, 1886.
Photographer: J.J. Williams.
Baker-Van Dyke Collection.

Palace guards and members of the Hawaiian
Militia in front of 'Iolani Palace. At left, in
white uniforms, the Royal Hawaiian Band.
Honolulu, 1882.
Photographer: H.L. Chase.
Hawai'i State Archives.

Assembly at a Kamehameha Day ceremony.
At extreme left is Oliver Stillman.
Honolulu, 1919.
Photographer: Unknown.
Bishop Museum.

Various Hawaiian Civic Clubs gather for a
Kamehameha Day ceremony.
Honolulu, 1919.
Photographer: Unknown.
Bishop Museum.

Various Hawaiian Civic Clubs gather for a
Kamehameha Day ceremony.
Honolulu, 1919.
Photographer: Unknown.
Bishop Museum.

Ka'ahumanu Society members in front of
the Kamehameha Statue.
Honolulu, circa 1920s.
Bishop Museum.

Descendants of chiefs of Hawai'i gather at Ford Island in Pearl Harbor at the estate of Charles Augustus "Cabby" Brown. Included are: Prince Kūhiō, Charles Augustus Brown, Judge George Davis, Kimo Wilder, Bob Shingle, Carl Hagens, Alexander Robinson, and Judge Stanley.
O'ahu, 1908.
Photographer: Edward P. Irwin.
Baker-Van Dyke Collection.

Queen Lili'uokalani's funeral procession.
Honolulu, 1917.
Photographer: Theodore Kelsey.
June Gutmanis Collection.

Mele a'me Hula / Music and Dance

Songs of the Hawaiian
people of old.
Rhythmic chants of
inspired poetry.
Empassioned compositions
Of life and myth,
Of chiefs and gods,
Of love, joy and sorrow.

HULA

Rhythmic dance of the
Hawaiian people.
Dance of ancient
Polynesian origin.
Ritualistic dance of the *kuahu* altar.
Dance of the *ōlapa*
who transformed
The *mele* song of the *ho'opa'a*
Into inspired poetry in motion.

Composed by Palani Vaughan

A student at the Kohala Girls Seminary.
Kohala, Hawai'i, 1912.
Photographer: Ray J. Baker.
Baker-Van Dyke Collection.

The *mele* was the traditional music of old Hawai'i, which Pūkui'i-Elbert defines as a "song, chant of any kind, poem." Although there were many categories of *mele* and various techniques and styles of chanting, most of the important *mele* dealt with the gods and chiefs.

Mele were chanted or sung by *ho'opa'a*, who accompanied themselves in a variety of ways such as on large *pahu* drums, on smaller knee drums called *pūniu*, on *ipu heke* gourds, or other forms of instrumental accompaniment.

Some *mele*, called *oli*, proscribed accompaniment of any kind including the *hula*. The singers of these chants were called *mea oli*. However, most *mele* allowed or even required *hula* complement by dancers called *'ōlapa*. *'Ōlapa* could enhance their choreography and the instrumentation of the *ho'opa'a* using a variety of dance implements, such as gourd rattles, called *'uli'uli* and *'ūlili*, *kāla'au* sticks, *papa hehi* treadle boards and other implements.

Prospective *ho'opa'a* and *'ōlapa* were assembled under the tutelage of a *hula* master into a school of *hula*, called *hālau hula*, in which all participants were required to observe strict rules of ritual conduct and purification during training. The focal point of the *hālau* was the altar, or *kuahu*, and the ceremonial *hula* performed there were termed *hula kuahu*. Some *hālau hula* were supported by royal patrons, who often became involved in the enterprise themselves.

King Kalaniopu'u, who hosted Captain Cook and his officers and men at the Makahiki Festival gatherings at his royal village site in Kealakekua Bay, Hawai'i, was a patron of the *hula* and often performed dances.

Later, King Kamehameha the Great scrutinized and adjusted the costumes of his royal *'ōlapa* before he allowed them to engage in a performance in honor of his guest and good friend, the British navigator Captain George Vancouver.

Finally, there was King Kalākaua, who as a child had received training in the art of chanting and *hula*. Later, as Hawai'i's ruler, he elevated traditional *hula* and *mele* as performing arts and fathered a period of creative activity that developed into a colorful and productive renaissance era of Hawaiian culture and arts. The revival of the *hula* was invigorated by innovations encouraged or initiated by the king, such as *hula ku'i*, the merging of old traditional steps with new foreign-inspired dance movements. The same was true of the king's approach to Hawaiian music. Perhaps the first foreign music heard by Hawaiians of old came from crew members aboard Captain Cook's exploratory ships and, most certainly, from sailors and passengers who arrived later aboard other visiting vessels from around the globe.

However, the melodic influence of western music would not impact Hawai'i until after the death of King Kamehameha the Great, with the arrival in 1820 of Boston missionaries singing inspired Christian hymns. In fact, it was the musical instruction provided by missionaries Mr. and Mrs. Amos Starr Cooke, through their Chiefs' Children's School, that would dramatically affect the lives of a particular family of Hawaiian royal children, the Kalākauas. That family not only served Hawai'i as its last ruling dynasty but also provided Hawai'i with one of its most lasting gifts to the world—the gift of song.

Born of the Kalākaua renaissance
era, modern forms of Hawaiian music
and dance emerged under royal
influence, while simultaneously, traditional *mele* and *hula* thrived under
the revivalist efforts of the Hawaiian
crown. Although they are credited
with having composed *mele* in the
traditional mode, King Kalākaua and
his younger siblings, Prince Leleiō-
Hoku and Princesses Lili'uokalani
and Likelike, are also recognized
as the first serious composers of
melodic Hawaiian songs.

This royal family of accom-
plished musicians and singers
ushered in a musical attitude that was
relatively new to Hawai'i and, through
their published songs, introduced a
new musical image of old Hawai'i to
the outside world.

These *ali'i* composers produced
songs of praise, romantic love and
love for the land in the form of
marches, hymns, ballads, waltzes
and *hula*-tempo tunes. The lyrics of
their songs contained references to
historic landmarks, legendary gods,
heroes and heroines from ancient
Hawaiian oral literature and famous
chiefs or rulers. For example, in
"Hawai'i Pono'ī," originally Hawai'i's
royal national anthem and now,
the state song of Hawai'i, the lyrics
acknowledge King Kamehameha I
as the Hawaiian Kingdom's Founding
Father. In *"Ninipo,"* reference is made
to the mythical woman Hōpoe, who
legend says was turned into stone
by the vengeful and enraged fire-
goddess, Pele.

Some sources indicate that the
Kalākauas even put melodies to old
mele chants, as Prince LeleiōHoku
reportedly did with *"Hole Waimea,"*
which was said to be one of the
name chants for the warrior King
Kamehameha the Great. The royal

Seated hula dancers in front of an unusual
grass house having a door, windows and a
front porch.
Hanalei, Kaua'i 1872.
Photographer: H.L. Chase.
Baker-Van Dyke Collection.

Backyard hula dancing on a rug atop
the grass.
Circa 1905.
Photographer: Alonzo Gartley.
Bishop Museum.

An enactment of old style hula with 1880s costumes (left) and 1860s costumes (right). In old Hawai'i, the hula was of basic significance and occupied a prominent place in the culture. Strict discipline and severe training of a religious nature were required of the dancers. The completion of the course of instruction was celebrated with appropriate graduation exercises.
Honolulu, 1914.
Photographer: Ray J. Baker.
Baker-Van Dyke Collection.

composers apparently felt that this musical approach would make a more lasting impression in people's minds and help to preserve, through music, these invaluable oral treasures which otherwise could be lost in the progress of change in Hawai'i.

Organized singing glee clubs, which on many occasions engaged in good-natured song competitions within their groups, helped to popularize the new compositions. Prince LeleiōHoku led Hui o Kawaihau Glee Club, noted for having the best singers and, reportedly, winning most of the sing-off contests.

While vocal harmonies were important, stringed instruments of foreign origin, such as the guitar, *'ukulele,* autoharp and others, enhanced the new Hawaiian melodies.

Their beautiful songs not only enriched the lives of their loyal subjects of that time, but also touched the souls of generations of Hawaiians and Hawaiians-at-heart here and abroad. Hauntingly sweet songs such as *"Aloha 'Oe,"* Lili'uokalani's moving tune of farewell that receives world acclaim today as it did in her time, is one example. The original music of the Kalākaua Dynasty has inspired the growth and development of Hawaiian musicianship, singing and

songwriting among the Hawaiians over the decades.

In creating musical accompaniments, early Hawaiian musicians deviated from accepted tuning standards by developing their own methods of tuning the guitar and *'ukulele,* which produced a distinctive plucking style called "slack-key," or *kī hō'alu.*

Another distinctively Hawaiian sound in guitar accompaniment was created through a playing technique invented by Hawaiian musician Joseph Kekuku, which led to the development of an instrument that became a gift to the musical world beyond Hawai'i . . . the steel guitar.

Today, Hawaiian musical gatherings continue as they did during the monarchal times under the Kalākaua family. Over the years, glee clubs of various kinds, numerous Hawaiian civic clubs and several high school choruses, such as the individual class choruses formed annually at Kamehameha Schools for Hawaiian children, have engaged in sing-off competitions. These contests are reminiscent of the Kalākaua Dynasty song contests . . . and one can still hear the haunting refrains of their beautiful music.

Today, the *'ukulele* and the guitar, whether "slack-key" tuned or "steel," continue as important elements of the Hawaiian sound. This is evident whether heard on recordings in live concerts, at *lū'au* feasts, or in Waikīkī hotel showrooms. Since the passing of the Hawaiian monarchy, generations of Hawaiian musicians, singers and dancers have carried on the musical traditions fostered at the end of the last century by the Kalākauas, from the revived form of traditional *mele* and *hula,* as performed by *hula* masters such as the late, great, 'Iolani Luahine, to the melodious songs of Hawai'i and its less restrictive *hula'auwana* accompaniment, as was humorously performed by the late Hilo Hattie, Hawai'i's great *hula* comedienne of international acclaim.

It is fitting in the Year of the Hawaiian that Hawaiian music and dance be recognized for its enriching influence on the quality of life, as it was in Hawai'i in days of old and as it is today. Hawai'i's musicians and dancers over the years have been important vehicles for the transmission of the Hawaiian heritage and culture from one generation to the next, and from Hawaiians to non-Hawaiians.

Hula girls in studio setting.
Honolulu, circa 1890s.
Photographer: J.J. Williams.
Hawaii State Archives.

In 1874, King Kalākaua wrote the "Hymn of Kamehameha I," now called "Hawai'i Pono'ī," to which Henry Berger composed the music.
Baker-Van Dyke Collection.

"Aloha 'Oe March" written in honor of the visit of Princess Lili'uokalani and Queen Kapi'olani to Boston on the way to Queen Victoria's Jubilee in 1887.
Baker-Van Dyke Collection.

Hula performance at King Kalākaua's 50th birthday jubilee.
Honolulu, November 1986.
Photographer: J.J. Williams.
Baker-Van Dyke Collection.

Chanter at the Mossman Hawaiian Village.
Honolulu, 1953.
Photographer: Ray J. Baker.
Bishop Museum.

The Bina Mossman Glee Club at the April
1927 opening of the Honolulu Academy of
Arts. Back row L to R: Helen Fuller, Kuʻualoha
Treadway, Flora Hayes, Gaelic Fitzgerald,
Emma Morreira. Front row L to R: Norma
Markham, Jenny Gilliland, Bina Mossman,
Elizabeth Bayless, Mary Saffery.
Honolulu, 1927.
Photographer: Tai Sing Loo.
Baker-Van Dyke Collection.

In 1874, King Kalākaua wrote the "Hymn of Kamehameha I," now called "Hawai'i Pono'ī," to which Henry Berger composed the music.

"Aloha 'Oe March" written in honor of the visit of Princess Lili'uokalani and Queen Kapi'olani to Boston on the way to Queen Victoria's Jubilee in 1887.

Hula performance at King Kalākaua's 50th birthday jubilee.
Honolulu, November 1986.
Photographer: J.J. Williams.

Ernest Ka'ai was a talented musician and composer. In old Hawai'i, there was great respect for the art of the composer and one of his manifold duties was to pass on his skill to the next generation. Composers had to be gifted persons with extensive knowledge of traditions and with inexhaustible amounts of information relating to place names, winds, rains and objects of nature.
Honolulu, circa 1910.
Photographer: Rice and Perkins.
Hawaiian Mission Children's Society.

Hula dancers in front of a backdrop of Hawaiian quilts at King Kalākaua's 50th Birthday Jubilee Lū'au.
Honolulu, November 16, 1886.
Photographer: Walter M. Gifford.
Baker-Van Dyke Collection.

Practicing a hula movement.
Honolulu, 1918.
Photographer: Bonine.
Baker-Van Dyke Collection.

Chanter at the Mossman Hawaiian Village.
Honolulu, 1953.
Photographer: Ray J. Baker.
Bishop Museum.

The Bina Mossman Glee Club at the April
1927 opening of the Honolulu Academy of
Arts. Back row L to R: Helen Fuller, Kuʻualoha
Treadway, Flora Hayes, Gaelic Fitzgerald,
Emma Morreira. Front row L to R: Norma
Markham, Jenny Gilliland, Bina Mossman,
Elizabeth Bayless, Mary Saffery.
Honolulu, 1927.
Photographer: Tai Sing Loo.
Baker-Van Dyke Collection.

Above: An old style musical interlude at the original Volcano House, now an art gallery. The lady at right is the famous Helen Desha Beamer.
Volcano, Hawai'i, 1928.
Photographer: Ray J. Baker.
Baker-Van Dyke Collection.

A hula group at the old Beamer house, "Hale Miku," in Hilo. Isabella Kalili Desha with gourd rattle. Baby Beamer is in front next to famed chanter Kuluwaimaka.
Hilo, Hawai'i, 1928.
Photographer: Ray J. Baker.
Baker-Van Dyke Collection.

'Iolani Luahine (1915-1979) first learned Hawaiian dancing at the age of three from her grandmother, Keahi, former dancer at the royal court. She continued her studies at the age of fourteen under Mary Kāwena Pūkuʻi, and made her professional debut as a solo dancer in 1947. She performed and taught during the rest of her life. In 1956, she was made curator of Huliheʻe Palace at Kailua, Kona. She retired as custodian of the Royal Mausoleum in Honolulu in 1965. In 1960, "Hoʻolauleʻa," a film demonstrating her art, was made by Francis Haar. During her life 'Iolani Luahine was considered the foremost preserver of the ancient Hawaiian dance repertory.
Photographer: Francis Haar.

Clarissa Haili (1901–1979), better known
as Hilo Hattie, the outstanding comic-hula
performer of her time, began entertaining as a
child, and sang in the choir of tiny Ke Alaula
o ka Mālamalama Church on Cooke Street.
In 1939, after teaching sixteen years at
Waipahu Elementary School, she joined
Harry Owens and his Royal Hawaiian
Serenaders in San Francisco. For almost thirty
years, "Aunty Clara" was a familiar figure in
her holoku and coconut hat, singing about
Princess Pupule and the Cockeyed Mayor of
Kaunakakai.

  She was photographed during a perfor-
mance in the Kodak Hula Show at San Souci.
Waikīkī, 1937.
Photographer: Ray J. Baker.
Baker-Van Dyke Collection.

"Aunt" Jennie Wilson (1873-1962), born
as Ana Kini Kapahuhula-o-Kamāmalu
Ku'ulalani, was a dancer at the court of King
Kalākaua. She joined a theatrical troupe in
1892 and toured the mainland and Europe,
performing for royalty and chiefs of state. She
married John Henry Wilson in 1908 and
moved to Pelekunu Valley, Moloka'i, to engage
in the growing of taro. She was a leader in the
'Ahahui Ka'ahumanu and when her husband
was mayor of Honolulu she was "honorary
first lady."
Honolulu, 1934.
Photographer: Ray J. Baker.
Baker-Van Dyke Collection.

Above: The Amphitheater stands and seating were especially built at the King Street entrance to ʻIolani Palace grounds. They are filled with people watching King Kalākaua's Coronation ceremony at the coronation stand called "Ke Liʻi Poni Hale."
Honolulu, February 12, 1983.
Photographer: Unknown.
Bishop Museum.

The art form of hula in this modern setting contrasts with a performance at King Kalākaua's Coronation at the same location about one hundred years earlier.
Honolulu, 1986.
Photographer: Douglas Peebles.

Ana ʻĀina / Cultural Celebrations

Composed by Palani Vaughan

Another type of less formal gathering in the Hawaiian community is the cultural celebration, which often occurs with much pageantry and ceremony. The longest and most notable of the ancient celebrations occurred from about the middle of October and lasted about four months, with sports and religious activities and a taboo on war. This celebration was called the *Makahiki* and was devoted to giving thanks to Lono, the god of fertility. In addition to the *Makahiki*, the people of old gathered together during the *ana ʻāina, anaina* or *anaina kānaka*. Andrews explains that the *anaina* in its most common usage was "an eating circle." However, he also defines it as "a congregation of people for any purpose, provided a space be left in the center; a congregation."

Similarly, Andrews states that *anaina*, as a verb, means "to assemble around a person or place; to meet around a thing." There have been throughout Hawaiʻi's history many large gatherings similar to the *Makahiki* and *anaina* of old Hawaiʻi when people assembled for serious ceremony, feasting, celebration, recreation and amusement. Many of these historic gatherings originated during the Kalākaua monarchal era when great attention was given to reviving Hawaiian pride and unity. King Kalākaua initiated a variety of *anaina* to celebrate the culture and art of Hawaiian heritage. The people responded with devotion to their king's efforts to animate national integrity.

Perhaps the king's greatest *anaina*, however, was the Royal Coronation in 1883 when he crowned himself and his wife Kapiʻolani the Supreme Rulers of the Kingdom. It was an unforgettable ceremony—a coronation of a Polynesian monarch with the pageantry of British Royal pomp, the piety of Christian ritual and the heritage of Hawaiian *aliʻi*. The dancing and music seemed endless; the feasting was sumptuous and the pride of the Hawaiian people was lifted to new heights.

In the Year of the Hawaiian, the community still looks to *anaina* to renew the bonds of ethnic unity among Hawaiians. The inauguration of Governor John Waiheʻe, Hawaiʻi's first elected Hawaiian governor, was a celebration of accomplishment and recognition. The successful completion of the *Hōkūleʻa's* "Voyage of Rediscovery" was welcomed with festivities and commemorations to the ancient skills of Polynesian navigators. In addition, the annual Merrie Monarch *hula* competitions in Hilo have been continual focal points for the striving of cultural excellence in the song, poetry and dance of the Hawaiian people.

As Hawaiians look toward tomorrow, they can take strength from their heritage of old. In their gatherings, they will continue to hear the voices on the wind carrying the words that have been so important to the spirit of the people, *ʻOhana, Keiki, Kūpuna, Kāne, Wāhine, Aliʻi, ʻAhahui, Anaina*. The language of old endures, bestowing love upon the new generations and guiding the course for the future.

Kalākaua's Jubilee, honoring his fiftieth birthday, on November 16, 1886, featured parades, tableaux, illuminations, fireworks, public lūʻaus and hula dancing. In this picture, the king and queen lead the way followed by Liliʻuokalani and her husband, John Dominis.
Honolulu, 1886.
Photographer: Unknown.
Hawaiʻi State Archives.

KING KALĀKAUA'S WORLD TOUR

The Hawaiian pride which King Kalākaua instilled in his people was repaid in the love and esteem they showed their beloved leader. Everywhere His Majesty traveled, large gatherings of natives dramatically displayed their respect and admiration for him with ceremony, prayers, chants and *hula.*

On January 20, 1981, native Hawaiians gathered in Honolulu to sing and dance praises to their king once again. King Kalākaua was scheduled to sail aboard the Australian steamer, *City of Sydney,* for San Francisco, California, on the first leg of his planned goodwill circumnavigation of the globe.

In fact, the traditional *mele,* or chant and *hula* could not end until the king sailed. The *City of Sydney* failed to arrive on time, delaying the king's departure; nevertheless, the people sustained their singing undeterred throughout the night until the *City of Sidney,* with their beloved king on board, steamed out of Honolulu Harbor at dawn the next day.

For most of that year, King Kalākaua journeyed far and wide, presenting a most favorable impression of Hawaiʻi and his people, even in his personal contacts with far more powerful and wealthier rulers and leaders, such as the Emperor of Japan and Queen Victoria of Great Britain.

On October 29, nine months after leaving his Kingdom, Kalākaua returned to his loving people. Relieved to be home at last, His Majesty delivered a moving address to his subjects, filled with humility, sincerity and deep gratitude for his good fortune:

"Ka Momi" (The Pearl)
Translated by Mary Kāwena Pūkuʻi
From: *Echo of Our Song*

I have traveled over many lands and
    distant seas, to India afar and
    China renowned.
I have touched the shores of Africa
    and the boundaries of Europe,
And I have met the great ones of all
    the lands.
As I stood at the side of heads of
    governments next to leaders
    proud of their rule, their
    authority over their own,
I realized how small and weak is the
    power I hold.
For mine is a throne established upon
    a heap of lava.
They rule where millions obey
    their commands.
Only a few thousand can I count
    under my care.
Yet one thought came to me of which
    I may boast, that of all beauties
    locked within the embrace of
    these shores,

One is a jewel more precious than
    any owned by my fellow
    monarchs.
I have nothing in my kingdom
    to dread.
I mingle with my people without fear.
My safety is no concern, I require no
    bodyguards,
Mine is the boast that a pearl of great
    price has fallen to me from above.
Mine is the loyalty of my people.

It is important in the Year of the Hawaiian to reflect on proud historic moments. And it is just as significant to remember meaningful events of this time that have given Hawaiʻi's people cause to congregate.

There have been a number of memorable *anaina* gatherings held this year which will be warmly remembered and treasured by future generations of Hawaiians. Of these, one *anaina* focused on what was probably the cultural highlight of the Year of the Hawaiian: the completion of the *Hōkūleʻa* "Voyage of Rediscovery" and return to Hawaiʻi, called "The Homecoming."

Above: King Kālakaua and his retinue
in Wailuku.
Photographer: H.L. Chase.
Bishop Museum.

The City of Honolulu gets ready to welcome
Kalākaua back from his first world tour, on
October 29, 1881.
Honolulu, 1881.
Photographer: Unknown.
Hawai'i State Archives.

Governor Waihe'e's Inauguration was well attended by foreign dignitaries, government officials and prominent members of communities throughout the state.
Photographer: Douglas Peebles

Members of 'Ahuahui Ka'ahumanu proudly watch the inauguration.
Photographer: Douglas Peebles.

Right: A proud Governor and his wife smile as they wave to well-wishers.
Photographer: Ken Sakamoto.
Star-Bulletin Photo.

THE INAUGURATION OF GOVERNOR WAIHE'E

On December 1, 1986, in an event generously flavored with traditional Hawaiian observances, chants, hula and music, Hawai'i's first elected governor of Hawaiian ancestry, John Waihe'e II, was inaugurated in a memorable ceremony attended by nearly ten thousand people, including foreign dignitaries, members of the Hawaiian community and the general public. The occasion was made even more memorable and symbolic because the Honorable John Waihe'e would have the distinction of serving his first year as governor of Hawai'i during the State of Hawai'i's observance of the Year of the Hawaiian.

In a February 17, 1987, Honolulu *Star-Bulletin* article, Governor Waihe'e would sum up his feelings concerning the great significance of the occasion.

"As the first elected Hawaiian governor, I clearly understand that I am a symbol of Hawaiian pride in what we are in the present, and what we can become in the future. I accept that role because I believe that Hawaiians provide the catalyst for all people in Hawai'i to join in the harmony, and as the ancient Hawaiians did, act as stewards for this precious chain of the islands. During 1987, I urge everyone, of every ancestry, to celebrate the Hawaiian with respect and sensitivity, and perhaps a renewed perspective of an old point of view. We need to recognize that in unity we are all *Ho'olako*—we are enriched, indeed, by one another."

Hālau Mohala ʻIlima performs.
Hilo, Hawaiʻi, April 14, 1985.
Photographer: Boone Morrison

Below: Nina Maxwell's Pukakani hula hālau.
Hilo, Hawaiʻi, April 14, 1985.
Photographer: Boone Morrison.

THE MERRIE MONARCH FESTIVAL

Each April since its founding by George Nā'ope and "Dottie" Thompson in 1963, the Merrie Monarch Festival and Hula Competition is held in Hilo, Hawai'i. It is attended by spectators and participants from all the islands as well as from the continental United States and other parts of the world.

The three-night event and competition celebrates and fosters the perpetuation of the hula and credits King Kalākaua, dubbed the "Merrie Monarch" during his reign, for reviving the open practice and display of this unique performing art form.

It was the king's request that on his coronation day on February 12, 1883, and again on his 50th Birthday Jubilee, on November 16, 1886, that there be massive hula performances extending over many days. These were to be the first public and free licensings of the hula in several decades. His Majesty Kalākaua is also credited with encouraging innovations to the hula.

"Johnny Lum Ho" hālau—Ka Ua Kani Lehua.
Hilo, Hawai'i, 1983.
Photographer: Boone Morrison.

THE RETURN OF THE HŌKŪLE'A

On the morning of May 23, 1987, thousands of joyous celebrants gathered at Windward O'ahu's historic Kualoa Beach Park to welcome the celebrated double-hulled voyaging canoe *Hōkūle'a*, home from its "Voyage of Rediscovery." The courageous crew and its young master navigator, Nainoa Thompson, were greeted with dignified ceremony, prayers, traditional chants and hula, and praises.

Thompson had received long and invaluable training in ocean navigation following the stars, the sun and the moon, and correctly interpreting ocean wave and cloud patterns from famed Micronesian master navigator Mau Piailug, who had successfully guided the double-hulled canoe on its first voyage in 1976 from Hawai'i to Tahiti.

Previous *Hōkūle'a* voyages were arranged and coordinated by the Polynesian Voyaging Society, which also devised this latest and most daring adventure into South Pacific waters. The society, which created *Hōkūle'a*, seeks to prove through a series of designed voyages that planned navigation by Pacific island peoples, particularly the early settlers of Hawai'i, occured over long distances and without instruments; that voyaging canoes like *Hōkūle'a* made it possible for Pacific island nations to initiate and sustain contact with each other; and that, in particular, it was possible for ancient Polynesians to sail in the face of prevailing winds from western to eastern Polynesia.

Hōkūle'a returned to its spiritual birthplace at Kualoa from this, its most challenging mission, the "Voyage of Rediscovery," after a two-year, 16,000-mile-long journey across the Pacific, retracing the ancient migratory routes of early Polynesians. *Hōkūle'a* originated this voyage in 1985 in Hawai'i when it sailed to Tahiti, the Cook Islands, New Zealand, Tonga, Sāmoa and back to the Cook Islands and Tahiti. After seven months in drydock, *Hōkūle'a* resumed the "Voyage of Rediscovery," sailing from Tahiti to Rangi Roa and finally, back to Hawai'i.

The society had devised the "Voyage of Rediscovery" as a project for all Polynesians and that purpose was effectively reflected in its crew, which consisted of representatives of nearly all of the Polynesian Island nations visited by *Hōkūle'a*.

The successful voyages of *Hōkūle'a* have enhanced the world's perception of the Hawaiian and Polynesian people, particularly their knowledge of navigation. The voyages have also helped to unify the spirit of Pacific islanders, who now realize that long ago the voyaging canoe played an important role in the early settlement of Polynesia by their ancestors, their *kūpuna*. Here in Hawai'i, *Hōkūle'a* has brought Hawaiians closer to understanding the origins of their ancestors.

Left: Hōkūleʻa returns from the sea.
"Thousands wade into the sea to greet the
Hokuleʻa as it prepares to land at Kualoa
beach (now renamed for the canoe). An altar
was erected at the clearing in the sand (left
of the canoe), where the crew sat for a traditional Hawaiian welcoming ceremony while
surrounded by the crowds."—Front Page,
the Sunday Star-Bulletin & Advertiser,
May 24, 1987.
Photographer: David Yamada.
Honolulu Advertiser.

Above: Micronesian navigator Mau Piaiʻlug
and Nainoa Thompson get a standing
ovation after receiving feather leis. At far right
is Kelii Tauʻa who conducted the ceremony.
In the background are Governor John
Waiheʻe, Representative Daniel Akaka and
Waiheʻeʻs son, John.
Honolulu, 1987.
Photographer. Carl Viti.
Honolulu Advertiser.

"The conch shell sounds, signalling the
beginning of the traditional ceremony."
—The Sunday Star-Bulletin & Advertiser.
Honolulu, May 24, 1987.
Photographer: Ron Jett.
Honolulu Advertiser.

Through its amazing feats over
the past eleven years and its proud
service to Hawaiʻi and Polynesia,
Hōkūleʻa has enriched the lives of
many people, including Hawaiians
and those of non-Hawaiian ancestry.

To honor *Hōkūleʻa* and its
crew for their success, Governor
John Waiheʻe proclaimed that Kualoa
Beach Park be officially renamed
Hōkūleʻa Beach Park.

HEAR ME, O' MY PEOPLE

An *anaina* of an unusual form has been the award-winning stage play *Hear Me, O' My People,* written by Donald Berrigan and starring veteran entertainer Marlene Sai. The drama portrays Queen Lili'uokalani a few weeks before her 77th birthday. Besides local perform-ances, there were showings in July of 1987 in Washington, D.C., before a special congressional audience. Through this dramatization, both Hawaiians and non-Hawaiians can better understand the tumultuous political forces faced by the queen and Hawai'i during a dark period in Hawaiian history.

Marlene Sai as Queen Lili'uokalani in a performance during the Association of Hawaiian Civic Clubs Convention in November, 1985.
Kihei, Maui.
Photo Credit: Maui News.

Index of Family Names

A

Lameka Ahu-lau, 99
Daniel Akaka, 172
Madame Alapaʻi, 112
Kaʻuhane ʻĀpiki, 73
Hoʻohuli ʻĀpiki, 73

B

Elizabeth Bayless, 160
Baby Beamer, 161
Helen Desha Beamer, 161
Mrs. Henry G. Bertleman, 92
James Boyd, 38
Charles Augustus Brown, 151

C

Mrs. Conradt, 113
John Cummins, 38

D

Judge George Davis, 151
Sam Dawlein, 43
Emma Defries, 102
Isabella Kalili Desha, 161

F

Gaelic Fitzgerald, 160
Mrs. Mary Fitzsimmons, 117
Helen Fuller, 160

G

Albert Gandall (family), 57
Antone Gasper (family), 57
Jenny Gilliland, 160

H

Carl Hagens, 151
John Haili Jr., 64
John Haili Sr., 64
Haliʻilehua, 106
Hilo Hattie, 163
Flora Hayes, 160
Ioane Hoʻa, 75
Daniel Hoʻolapa (family), 49

I

Iʻaukea (family), 51
Curtis Iʻaukea, 51
Judge John Papa ʻĪʻī, 68
Victoria ʻIkuwā, 106
Inoka Makahanaloa, 98

K

Ernest Kaai, 158
David Kaʻapu, 95
Maria Merseberg Kahaʻi, 39
Bill Kahanamoku, 96
David Kahanamoku, 96
Duke Kahanamoku, 96, 97
Louis Kahanamoku, 96
Sam Kahanamoku, 96
Sargent Kahanamoku, 96
Mrs. William Kaʻimieka, 69
David Kaiwa Jr., 131
David Kaiwa Sr., 131
Mrs. Mileka Kalaʻau and children, 65
Kalua, 106
Charles K. Kamahoahoa (family), 56
Robert William Kamakahi Jr. (family), 58
Mrs. Louise Kāne (family), 53
Oliver Kaniau, 106
John Kuualoha Kaohelaulii, 123
Naʻauao Kaʻōpūiki, 98
Noa Kaopuiki, 59
Kapehekawelo, 106
Abraham Kauila, 98
James Kauila, 100
David Kawai (family), 59
Kawika Shintani, 123
John Maliko Kekua (family), 63
Kiaania, 66
Joseph H. Kīʻaha, 72
Mr. & Mrs. John T. Kīkoʻo (and granddaughter), 75
Mrs. Hulia Kipopa (family), 51
S.W. Kīʻuo, 69
Mrs. Kūhiō, 71
Kauhane Kukololua, 71
Kuluwaimaka, 160, 161

L

ʻIolani Luahine, 162
Phillip Luahiwa, 132
Mrs. Carrie Luhiau (family), 56

M

William Maertens (family), 65
Kameaeokalani Māhoe, 145
Kaliko Makakoa, 100
David Malo, 94
Norma Markham, 160
Margaret K. Martin, 92
Dan Meheʻula (family), 60
Emma Morreira, 160
Bina Mossman, 160

N

Kalua-Ahi Nu, 106

P

Paʻalani, 74
Mau Piailug, 173
Governor Pinkham, 141
James Pōʻahā (family), 55
Mrs. William F. Pogue (family), 54
Mrs. John Porter, 113

R

Alexander Robinson, 151

S

Mary Saffery, 160
Marlene Sai, 174
Bob Shingle, 151
Judge Stanley, 151
Oliver Stillman, 148

T

Kelii Tauʻa, 172
Nainoa Thompson, 172
Samuel K. Toomey (family), 63
Kuʻualoha Treadway, 160

W

Wilmot Vredenburg, 72
Mrs. Wilmot Vredenburg, 72
John Waiheʻe, 168, 172
Lynne Waiheʻe, 168
John Waiheʻe III, 172
Kimo Wilder, 151
"Aunt" Jennie Wilson, 163

Lorrin Andrews. *A Dictionary of the Hawaiian Language.*
Rutland, Vermont, 1974: Charles E. Tuttle Co., Inc.

A. Grove Day. *History Makers of Hawaii: A Biographical Dictionary.*
Honolulu, 1984: Mutual Publishing.

Nathaniel B. Emerson. *Unwritten Literature of Hawai'i.*
Rutland, Vermont, 1977: Charles E. Tuttle Co., Inc.

Joseph Feher. *Hawai'i: A Pictorial History.*
Honolulu, 1969: Bishop Museum Press.

Jerry Hopkins. *The Hula.*
Hong Kong, 1982: APA Productions (Hong Kong), Ltd.

Ralph S. Kuykendall. *The Hawaiian Kingdom,
Vol. III, 1874–1893, The Kalākaua Dynasty.*
Honolulu, 1967: The University Press of Hawai'i.

Kathleen Dickenson Mellon. *An Island Kingdom Passes.*
New York, 1958: Hastings House.

Mary Kāwena Pūku'i and Samuel H. Elbert. *Hawaiian Dictionary.*
Honolulu, 1986. The University Press of Hawai'i.

Mary Kāwena Pūku'i, Samuel H. Elbert and Esther T. Mo'okini.
Place Names of Hawai'i. Honolulu, 1974: The University Press of Hawai'i.

Mary Kāwena Pūku'i and Alfons L. Korn. *The Echo of our Song.*
Honolulu, 1973: The University Press of Hawai'i.

Kristin Zambucka. *Kalākaua: Hawai'i's Last King.* Honolulu, 1983:
Mana Publishing Co. and Marvin/Richards Enterprises, Inc.

Nā Leo i ka Makani
....
Voices on the Wind

Produced by Bennett Hymer, David Rick
and Gaylord Wilcox

Art direction by Bill Fong and
Leo Gonzalez

Designed by Veronica Lam

Design assistants: Leslie Charpentier
and Tamara Moan

Typesetting by Kellyjean Evans

Headline Type: Snell Roundhand Script
and Futura Bold Condensed
Test and Caption Type: Berkeley Book
and Berkeley Book Italic

Printed and bound in Tokyo, Japan by
Toppan Printing Co., Ltd.